# Making Sense of Mathematics

## Children Sharing and Comparing Solutions to Challenging Problems

*by*

Larry Buschman
Jefferson Elementary School
Jefferson, Oregon

NATIONAL COUNCIL OF
TEACHERS OF MATHEMATICS

Library of Congress Cataloging-in-Publication Data

Buschman, Larry.
  Making sense of mathematics : children sharing and comparing solutions to challenging
problems / by Larry Buschman.
     p. cm.
  Includes bibliographical references.
  ISBN-13: 978-0-87353-597-7
  ISBN-10: 0-87353-597-9
  1. Mathematics—Study and teaching (Elementary) 2. Problem solving—Study and teaching
(Elementary) I. National Council of Teachers of Mathematics.  II. Title.
QA135.6.B865 2007
372.7'044—dc22
                              2006035503

The National Council of Teachers of Mathematics is a public voice of mathematics education,
providing vision, leadership, and professional development to support teachers in ensuring
mathematics learning of the highest quality for all students.

Printed in the United States of America

# Contents

# Introduction

Past attempts to improve children's problem solving abilities in mathematics have primarily focused on (1) *better problems* for students to solve, leading to numerous books filled with nonroutine and open-ended problems, (2) *better strategies* for students to use when solving problems, resulting in several books promoting instruction in heuristics and problem-solving strategies, and (3) *better assessment tools* for teachers to use, leading to various books on portfolios and scoring rubrics. A more recent innovation for improving children's problem-solving abilities has focused on the creation of a classroom culture that encourages students to solve challenging problems, work in cooperative learning groups, and discuss different ways of solving problems (NCTM 2000).

Although the major topics of curriculum content and assessment are important when discussing a problem-solving approach to mathematics instruction, the topics discussed in this book are equally important to ensure that a classroom mathematics curriculum centered on problem solving is (1) usable by both teachers and students and (2) effective in helping children acquire both content knowledge and problem-solving skills. As the cartoon below illustrates, sometimes small things can make a big difference—and this statement seems to be especially true when it comes to learning how to solve problems in mathematics.

This book examines the following topics, which have not received a great deal of attention from other authors: (1) posing and solving problems in a non-paper-and-pencil environment, (2) the role of student interviews in a problem-centered classroom, (3) how a multiage classroom can enhance children's problem-solving behaviors, (4) the developmental stages of young problem solvers, (5) the importance of positive dispositions and cognitive dissonance when solving problems, and (6) dispelling some of the myths about problem solving.

The first chapter is titled "Our School, Our Classroom, Our Explorations." This chapter describes the setting in which the children in a multiage classroom explore, solve, and discuss a wide range of mathematical problems. It provides a backdrop for examining various issues surrounding the teaching of problem solving that are examined in chapters 2–10 of this book.

Chapter 2 presents an overview of an instructional approach called *share and compare*. This approach is used by the children in the author's classroom to investigate and discuss solutions to challenging mathematical problems.

Chapter 3 contains an in-depth examination of children's solutions to non-paper-and-pencil problems that ask children to predict the weight of wooden unit blocks using a balance and nonstandard units of measurement. Although the quality of problems used in mathematics classrooms has improved dramatically over the past few years, problem solving remains primarily a paper-and-pencil activity. Much of this book (chapters 3 and 4) is devoted to the examination of children's responses to non-paper-and-pencil tasks in which the teacher poses problems using concrete objects and children solve the problems using the same objects along with their own intellectual abilities as young problem solvers. Non-paper-and-pencil problems are important for several reasons: (1) unlike traditional word (story) problems, they provide children with hands-on problem-solving experiences that more closely resemble problems found in the real world, and (2) unlike traditional word (story) problems that children sometimes solve while working alone at their desks, children solve and discuss these non-paper-and-pencil problems while in the company of their peers. As Kathy Richardson has noted,

> The young child's most important work is not going to appear on paper. It comes, rather, from engagement in activities. While children's beginning attempts to put their thinking down on paper can be of interest, their products do not reveal what is most important about their developing understanding.... We need instead to plan experiences that support the development of the mathematical concepts we want our children to work with and then observe and make note of our children at work.
>
> (Richardson 1997a, p. 100)

Chapter 4 continues the examination of children's solutions to non-paper-and-pencil problems. Children solve problems similar to those presented in chapter 3, by predicting the number of pattern blocks that will balance a wooden unit block. This chapter takes a further look at children's talents as problem solvers and at their unique ways of thinking mathematically, which often differ significantly from the ways adults think.

Chapter 5 takes a second look at the activities described in chapters 3 and 4. This chapter examines how seemingly minor changes in the way problems are presented to children can affect children's ability to successfully solve them.

Chapter 6 discusses why multiage classrooms are important in helping children become better problem solvers in mathematics. Both the social and academic benefits of an apprentice approach to instruction are discussed in this chapter.

Chapter 7 discusses the developmental stages of young children as they progress from beginning problem solvers to more advanced practitioners. This chapter guides teachers as they attempt to analyze children's performance as problem solvers, and helps teachers select the kind of support that will be most beneficial to children at each stage of their development.

Chapter 8 investigates the importance of positive dispositions in promoting successful problem-solving behaviors in the classroom. The chapter is based on comments made by children as they describe what teachers can do to promote beneficial and useful attitudes toward problem solving in the mathematics classroom. As the author notes, these dispositions seem to have the most lasting, long-term effect on children's ability to grow as successful problem solvers.

Chapter 9 explores the use of cognitive dissonance to promote a sense of inquisitiveness in the classroom. Rather than correct students' misconceptions through direct *teaching-by-telling,* the author suggests that teachers give students the appropriate support and encouragement to find their own answers to questions they find intriguing.

Chapter 10 attempts to dispel some of the past and present myths that surround the teaching of problem solving. This chapter describes how those myths distort discussions about the role of problem solving in mathematics reform, and undermine the efforts of teachers to help children become better problem solvers.

Each chapter is based on the author's personal observations and interactions with children in his classroom. As such, the book is not meant to be a *how to* book but rather an *about* book—a book about children answering challenging questions, and about teachers learning the art of questioning. As Albert Einstein observed,

> Most teachers waste their time by asking questions which are intended to discover what a pupil does not know, whereas the true art of questioning has for its purpose to discover what the pupil knows or is capable of knowing.
>
> (Einstein, 1879–1955)

# Our School, Our Classroom, Our Explorations

Problem solving is an integral part of all mathematics learning.
—National Council of Teachers of Mathematics
*Principles and Standards for School Mathematics*

IMAGINE students enthusiastically exploring a sequence of mathematics activities that is—

- based on a dilemma encountered by the children themselves in the course of an exploration,

- intriguing and motivating to the children because of their "ownership" of the problems being investigated, and

- sufficiently rich to fulfill the curriculum requirements of the school district and state.

Did such a scenario occur in a classroom of gifted and talented students? In a school in an affluent community? This scenario did occur—in fact, is occurring on a daily basis—in a classroom that is perhaps the antithesis of an imagined "ideal" setting.

## Our School and School District

The activities described in this book took place in a rural public school with approximately 400 children in grades K–4. The class structure comprised three half-day kindergarten classes (20 children per class), three multiage first-second-grade classes (30 children per class), three multiage first-second-third-grade classes (31 children per class), one multiage third-fourth-grade class (31 children), and four looped third-fourth-grade classes (31 children per class). In addition, two special education programs, a Head Start Program and an Early Childhood Intervention Program, were housed in the school. The school had been a Title 1 School since 1997 because of the high poverty rate in the area served by the school district. The student body was 76 percent white, 22 percent Hispanic, 1 percent American Indian, and 1 percent black. The school had one computer laboratory equipped with fifteen state-of-the-art computers having high-speed Internet access, and each classroom had one computer with Internet access.

The school district was composed of one elementary school, a middle school (grades 5–8), and a high school (grades 9–12). Although once a small farming community, the town had become a bedroom community for nearby larger cities. Alcohol and drug abuse were endemic because of high unemployment and the lack of a city police department. Quality child care was limited, and many children were often cared for by older siblings.

## Our Classroom

All the activities described in this book were conducted by the author during the 2002–2003 school year in a self-contained, multiage first-second-third-grade classroom (fig. 1.1). The classroom was well stocked with mathematics manipulatives, which the children used as tools to model mathematics problems and represent their solutions.

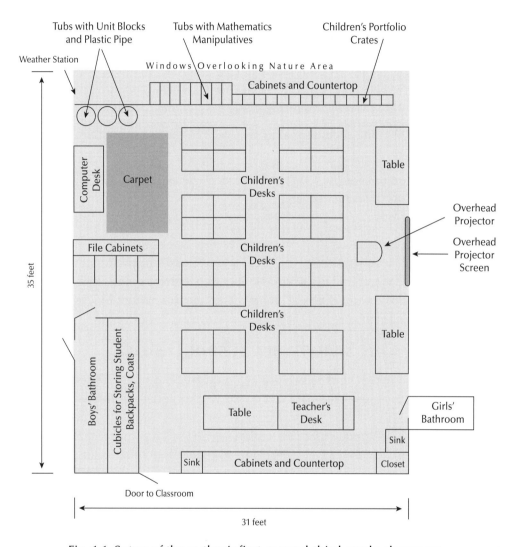

Fig. 1.1. Setup of the author's first-second-third-grade classroom

## The Teacher

The author has taught in the same school for twenty-seven years: fourteen years in single-grade classrooms (sixth, third, or second grade), three years in split-grade classrooms (second-third grade), and most recently ten years in multiage classrooms (first-second-third grade). He has discovered that a multiage approach has several advantages over the traditional single-grade classroom structure—one of which is the ability to help children become problem solvers in mathematics by fostering rich classroom discourse among children with a wide range of academic abilities and communication skills. A more complete description of how a multiage class can support and facilitate children's growth as problem solvers appears in chapter 6.

# The Children

The children who appear in the following chapters were all from the author's multiage class, which consisted of eleven first graders, ten second graders, and ten third graders. The fifteen girls and sixteen boys ranged in age from six to nine years and represented a broad range of academic abilities (twelve children had Individual Educational Plans for various learning disabilities, and two children were identified as talented and gifted). Twenty-six children were white (non-Hispanic), five were Hispanic, and one was African-American. Eleven children came from single-parent households, and one child was in foster care.

# Our Discussion Problems

The problems described in chapters 3 and 4 were based on discoveries that the children had made while exploring the use of a balance to weigh objects using standard and nonstandard units of measurement. These problems were designed to initiate productive discussions between small groups of children and the author. During the small-group discussions, children used a balance to predict how many glue sticks, plastic cubes, or pattern blocks would balance various wooden blocks.

The wooden blocks used during these discussions are commonly called Unit Blocks, which were designed by Caroline Pratt in 1948 while she was a teacher at the City and Country School in New York City (Hirsch 1996). Unit Blocks are cut so that the thickness of each block is the same, and the multiples and divisions of the *unit block* are exact. Ms. Pratt never named the blocks, so today they are usually sold under the manufacturer's name. Unit Blocks have become a common feature in primary school classrooms, and they are a favorite building material of children.

The problems used during the discussions can be characterized as open-ended and nonroutine because they can be solved in more than one way and they are not the typical computation-based word (story) problems that children are often asked to solve. In addition, the problems represent the author's attempt to find a middle ground between the extremes of direct instruction and discovery learning. By combining direct skills instruction with carefully designed problems and well-orchestrated discussions, the author has attempted to meet the needs of children to explore topics of interest to them while addressing the curriculum requirements of his school district and state (Appendix 1).

During the children's explorations with the balances, two of the children made a perplexing discovery. To their dismay and puzzlement, they became aware of an irregularity in their measurement results. To the author's surprise and the children's frustration, the children discovered that the weights of individual Unit Blocks were not proportional to their size. Thus a block that was twice as big as another block did not weigh twice as much. In fact, the weight of identical Unit Blocks was not consistent. The source of this dilemma soon became apparent to the author: it resided in the fact that the blocks were made of wood that did not have uniform *density*.

# Our Explorations

Faced with the nonproportionality dilemma, the author developed three different types of activities that either eliminated the discrepancies in the weights of the blocks or minimized their effects:

- One type of activity used standard wooden Unit Blocks. For this activity the author asked the children to use the weight of one Unit Block to predict the weight of other blocks. This approach effectively allowed the children to ignore the density dilemma during the activity because they were not actually weighing each block or using the balance to verify their predictions. Chapters 3 and 4 contain descriptions of the discussions among children using this type of activity.

- A second type of activity was similar to the first, but instead of using wooden blocks, the children used foam Unit Blocks. The foam blocks have a more uniform density than their wooden counterparts, and the children could verify most of their predictions even though minor irregularities were found in the weights of some blocks.

- The third type of activity used computer-simulated balances. This version of the activity eliminated all the variables present in the use of the real blocks and balances in the classroom. The main disadvantages of the computer-simulated balances were that they presented an activity that could not be modified to meet the specific abilities of the children in the classroom, nor could they be made to duplicate the types of investigations the children had chosen to explore.

As mentioned previously, the activities described in chapters 3 and 4 used standard wooden Unit Blocks and pattern blocks. The author chose to include only a description of those activities for several reasons:

- Doing so adds simplicity and clarity to the text of the book and gives a single focus to the purpose of the activities used with the children.

- Other teachers may want to replicate these activities, and teachers are more likely to have standard, wooden Unit Blocks and pattern blocks available in their classrooms than the other types of blocks mentioned previously.

- Standard, wooden Unit Blocks and pattern blocks fulfilled the main purpose of the activities, which was to encourage children to develop relationships between the size of the blocks and their weight, and to use logic to make sense of those relationships. In addition, by not being asked to actually verify their predictions during the activity, the children were challenged to offer support for their predictions rather than rely on the balance to tell them whether their predictions were correct. Accordingly, the children had to search out reasons for their suppositions, construct explanations that others would find understandable, and think more deeply about the conjectures of their classmates.

# 2

# An Overview of the
# Share-and-Compare Method
## Sharing to Learn, Learning to Share

The greatest compliment that was ever paid me was when someone asked me what I thought, and attended to my answer.

*—Henry David Thoreau*

Once a rabbi spoke with the Lord about Heaven and Hell, "I will show you Hell," said the Lord and they went into a room which had a large pot of stew in the middle. The smell was delicious and around the pot sat people who were famished and desperate. All were holding spoons with very long handles which reached to the pot, but because the handles of the spoons were longer than their arms, it was impossible to get the stew into their mouths. Their suffering was terrible.

"Now I will show you Heaven," said the Lord, and they went into an identical room. There was the same pot of stew and the people had the same identical spoons, but they were well-nourished, talking, and happy. At first the rabbi did not understand. "It is simple," said the Lord. "You see, they have learned to feed each other."

*—Jewish parable*

IN OUR classroom, the process children use to solve problems and share their solutions with one another is called *share and compare* (Buschman 2003). "Share and compare" is more than an instructional approach; it is a tool that children use to examine different solutions to problems, discuss the logic behind their solutions, and reflect on why some solutions make sense mathematically whereas others do not. It is a culture of discourse that children create to explore problem-solving strategies and mathematical concepts using creative and critical thinking, collaboration, and communication. As described in the National Council of Teachers of Mathematics' *Principles and Standards for School Mathematics*,

Communication is an essential part of mathematics and mathematics education. It is a way of sharing ideas and clarifying understanding. Through communication ideas become objects of reflection, refinement, discussion, and amendment. The communication process also helps build meaning and permanence for ideas and makes them public. When students are challenged to think and reason about mathematics and to communicate the results of their thinking to others orally or in writing, they learn to be clear and convincing. Listening to others' explanations gives students opportunities to develop their own understandings. (NCTM 2000, p. 60)

## Strengths of Share and Compare

When children fill in the blanks on drill-and-practice worksheets or engage in teacher-directed manipulative exercises, they have little to talk about when they are finished. About the only thing they and their teacher can discuss is whether the answers are the same or match the answer in the teacher's manual. By contrast, when children are asked to solve real problems—problems for which the answer is not apparent or the solution process is not known in advance—the mathematics classroom becomes a public forum where children discuss and analyze their classmates' uniquely individual approaches for solving problems. Children who participate in solving *challenging* problems have something genuine to talk about, and they can use those conversations to nourish one another intellectually. When children share their individual solutions, they feed one another new ideas and expose one another to new ways of thinking about familiar concepts. In addition, sharing solutions nourishes children socially by providing them with a way to collaborate with their peers in an academic setting.

Sharing and comparing solutions creates a community in which everyone benefits by the actions of others—including teachers. When children share and compare their solutions to problems, teachers discover what makes sense to children, and they are better able to give children the kind of feedback that children can use to clarify conceptual misunderstandings or improve their performance as budding mathematicians.

The major strengths of the share-and-compare approach include the following:

- It can be used at any grade level.
- It can be used in any classroom without the purchase of special materials or supplies.
- It can be used to ensure that classroom mathematics instruction incorporates the NCTM's five Process Standards: Problem Solving, Reasoning and Proof, Communication, Connections, and Representation (NCTM 2000).

## Core Beliefs and Practices of Share and Compare

The share-and-compare approach is based on four core beliefs and five core practices.

## Core Beliefs

- Mathematics is primarily a sense-making activity, and children can learn to make sense of mathematics through problem solving.

- Children can learn how to become problem solvers by participating in a learning community whose members solve problems in ways that make sense to them, share solutions with one another, and provide one another with useful feedback.

- Children can learn how to be members of a problem-solving community through reflection, self-assessment, and the gradual acquisition of the dispositions of a good problem solver.

- Children can learn reflection, self-assessment, and the dispositions of a good problem solver through a balanced assessment program that includes direct observation, student interviews, rubrics, and portfolios.

## Core Practices

- Children solve challenging problems in ways that makes sense to them. "At all grade levels, students should see and expect that mathematics makes sense" (NCTM 2000, p. 56).

- Children share their solutions with a partner. "Students need opportunities to test their ideas on the basis of shared knowledge in the mathematical community of the classroom to see whether they can be understood and if they are sufficiently convincing." (NCTM 2000, p. 61)

- Children tell why they agree or disagree with their partner's solution.

    From children's earliest experiences with mathematics, it is important to help them understand that assertions should always have reasons. Such questions as "Why do you think it is true?" and "Does anyone think the answer is different, and why do (they) think so?" help students see that statements need to be supported or refuted by evidence. (NCTM 2000, p. 56)

- Children share their solutions in small groups and receive feedback in the form of questions or comments.

    Through communication, ideas become objects of reflection, refinement, discussion, and amendment. The communication process also helps build meaning and permanence for ideas and makes them public. When students are challenged to think and reason about mathematics and to communicate the results of their thinking to others orally or in writing, they learn to be clear and convincing. (NCTM 2000, p. 60)

- Children compare several solutions with one another. "Conversations in which mathematical ideas are explored from multiple perspectives help the participants sharpen their thinking and make connections" (NCTM 2000, p. 60).

Although the foregoing beliefs and practices are easy to describe, they are hard for many teachers to implement because they represent a fundamentally different way of teaching and learning mathematics. In our society the traditional approach to teaching mathematics is not just an instructional model; it has acquired the status of an *institution* that is accepted by many people as the *only* way to teach mathematics. Because many people expect mathematics to be taught that way, they are not easily convinced that children can learn mathematics using a different approach.

As the reader will see from the description of the activities in the following chapters, young children can be accomplished problem solvers who like to talk about mathematics and the methods they use to solve challenging problems. For these children doing mathematics means crafting procedures for solving problems, explaining their procedures to one another, responding to questions or comments about their procedures, fine-tuning their procedures to meet the challenges of new problems, and reflecting on the procedures of others.

## Main Components of a Share-and-Compare Lesson

When used with children in small discussion groups, the share-and-compare model consists of four main components:

- Warm-up

- Solving problems and sharing solutions

- Comparing solutions

- Embedding skills development within problem-solving activities

These four main components of a share-and-compare lesson provide children with a framework that supports their efforts to become problem solvers. When children are given "time to talk, write, model, and draw pictures, as well as occasions for work in small groups, large groups, and as individuals, students who [work] best in different ways all [have] opportunities to learn" (NCTM 2000, p. 197).

### Warm-Up

The warm-up helps children acquire the conventions of mathematics through mental mathematics exercises that relate directly to the problem-solving portion of the lesson. For example, the warm-ups for the activities described in chapters 3 and 4 included discussions about (1) the characteristics of the Unit Blocks, (2) the names and characteristics of pattern block shapes, and (3) the meanings of some mathematical terms (*face, side, prediction, twice, one-half, balance,* and *scale*).

### Solving Problems and Sharing Solutions

Children solve problems in ways that make sense to them. They work on problems individually or with a partner, using the problem-solving tools that are available to them in the classroom.

The goals of the problems are to challenge children to think mathematically in many different contexts and situations, and to provide a rich source of material for discussion.

Next the children share their solutions and tell why they agree or disagree with one another. Children share their solutions to problems much in the same manner that Donald Graves recommends that children share literary pieces they have authored (Graves 1985). As described by Graves, offering children a public forum to share and discuss original stories, poems, and essays gives children a chance to compare their work with that of their peers and encourages children to provide feedback to one another. When children share solutions they have crafted for mathematics problems, they receive comparable benefits by improving their numeracy skills instead of their literacy skills. When sharing solutions, children are expected to use effective speaking skills and to communicate their thoughts clearly and completely. When listening to others, children are expected to use effective listening skills and to provide the person who is sharing with useful, respectful feedback. This feedback can address such questions as these:

- What did you like about the solution to the problem?

- Do you agree or disagree with the solution, and why?

- How could the solution be improved?

- How could the solution be changed to arrive at a new way of solving the problem?

When children are sharing solutions and strategies, the teacher's role is to facilitate the discussions by clarifying terminology or asking questions to deepen children's understanding of the mathematics concepts and ideas involved in the problems.

## Comparing Solutions

Children compare solutions by examining similarities or differences among them. With young children, this part of the lesson can be omitted or included only when it seems appropriate for particular problems and solutions. Judicious use or omission of this step helps keep the activity moving and the children focused.

## Embedding Skills Development within Problem-Solving Activities

Rather than teach skills in isolation, teachers can embed them within problem-solving activities. When planning problem-solving activities, I recommend that teachers try to anticipate the kinds of solutions that children are most likely to propose, then prepare themselves to be ready to *seize the teachable moment* and use children's comments or solution strategies as springboards for short minilessons on mathematics skills. Examples of such minilessons appear throughout the discussions in chapters 3 and 4.

# Concerns Teachers May Have about Share and Compare

## Use of Time

Using a share-and-compare approach can raise some concerns in the minds of teachers, and one of those concerns is the efficient and effective use of classroom time. Sometimes teachers think that they are faced with an either-or choice—that they can use their limited amount of mathematics instruction time either to do skills development or to do problem solving. This concern is legitimate because problem-solving activities are time-consuming, and time is a valued commodity in United States schools faced with high-stakes tests that hold teachers and schools accountable for children's performance.

Each of the small-group discussions described in chapters 3 and 4 lasted for about thirty minutes to one hour. This may seem like a long time for children to be solving a relatively few problems when one considers the amount of drill-and-practice exercises they could have completed in the same amount of time. Crafting solutions to problems unquestionably takes time, and sharing solutions takes even more time. But as James Hiebert and his colleagues have noted, problem solving and mathematical understanding are directly connected.

> If we want students to understand mathematics, it is more helpful to think of understanding as something that results from solving problems, rather than something we can teach directly.... It is more appropriate to engage students in solving problems because it is only through solving problems that their concepts and procedures develop together and remain connected in a natural and productive way. (Hiebert et al. 1997, p. 25)

In addition, instruction in basic skills and problem solving can occur simultaneously by teaching basic skills within the context of problem-solving activities, as described in chapters 3 and 4.

## Effectiveness of Problem-Solving Strategies

Teachers are also concerned about the practice of allowing children to solve problems in ways that make sense to children. Inventing their own approaches may seem to be an ineffective way for children to acquire problem-solving strategies, especially since well-developed programs are available for teaching children strategies, such as guess and check, work backward, look for a pattern, and so on. Although teaching children problem-solving strategies may seem like a logical thing to do, it suffers from the same shortcomings as teaching children basic skills though drill and practice—the problem-solving strategies must be constantly reviewed if children are to commit them to memory and use them appropriately in problem-solving situations. Also, every time children encounter a different kind of problem, they must be taught a new strategy. Teaching children problem-solving strategies robs them of the opportunity to do real problem solving—that is, to complete tasks "for which the solution method is not known in advance" (NCTM 2000, p. 52). As described by James Hiebert and others,

Students develop mathematical understanding as they invent and examine methods for solving problems. This is quite different than the usual claim which says that students acquire understanding as they listen to clear explanations by the teacher and watch the teacher demonstrate how to solve problems. (Hiebert at al. 1997, p. 17)

# What Research Says

Research shows that teaching students problem-solving strategies does little to advance their aptitude to solve mathematics problems in general. In fact, many of the programs used to teach those strategies are based not on sound research but rather on the assumption that novice problem solvers need to be familiar with the strategies used by experts (Lester 1994; Schoenfeld 1992). However, more recent research on problem solving has shown that children can and will invent their own strategies for solving problems. Instead of focusing on the *best ways* to teach problem-solving strategies, this research has found that the most effective way to facilitate children's growth as problem solvers is to build on their natural problem-solving abilities (Burns 1992; Buschman 2003, Carpenter et al. 1999; Mills, O'Keefe, Nelson, and Whitin 1996; Trafton and Thiessen 1999).

# Outcomes of Experience

On the basis of my experiences, the real question is not whether children should be taught problem-solving strategies but rather how and when this instruction should occur. Children should be exposed to traditional problem-solving strategies as one more way of solving problems rather than be taught that traditional strategies are the *only* way problems should be solved. Thus, "mathematics teaching in the lower grades should encourage students' [invented] strategies and [then] build on them as ways of developing more-general ideas and systematic approaches" (NCTM 2000, p. 76).

I should also mention that ten years ago our school decided to teach problem-solving strategies to children. At the time, that approach was recommended by many experts, and it was a natural extension of the traditional model of instruction we used. We thought such instruction would be a good way for children to acquire the strategies they needed to become successful problem solvers. At first, we were encouraged by the results—some children did learn how to solve some problems, but most children did not become problem solvers who could solve new or unusual problems. After using that approach for about three years, we eventually realized that teaching problem-solving strategies did not help young children acquire the characteristics and dispositions of confident and capable problem solvers.

# 3

# Predicting the Weight of Wooden Unit Blocks Using Nonstandard Units of Measurement
## Discussing to Learn, Learning to Discuss

If [students] spend most of their time practicing paper-and-pencil skills on sets of worksheet exercises, they are likely to become faster at executing these skills. If they spend their time watching the teacher demonstrate methods for solving special kinds of problems, they are likely to become better at imitating these methods on similar problems. If they spend most of their time reflecting on the way things work, on how various ideas and procedures are the same or different, on how what they already know relates to the situations they encounter, they are likely to build new relationships. That is, they are likely to construct new understandings. How they spend their time is determined by the tasks that they are asked to complete. The tasks make all the difference....

A person understands when he or she can communicate in a way that helps others understand.

—James Hiebert and others
*Making Sense: Teaching and Learning
Mathematics with Understanding*

Tʜᴇ National Council of Teachers of Mathematics' *Principles and Standards for School Mathematics states*, "Being able to reason is essential to understanding mathematics" (NCTM 2000, p. 56). That document goes on to say, "Building on the considerable reasoning skills that children bring to school, teachers can help students learn what mathematical reasoning entails" (NCTM 2000, p. 56). Therefore, the activities described in this book challenge children to apply their reasoning skills to the solution of nonroutine, open-ended, non-paper-and-pencil problems.

## Fostering Young Students' Emerging Reasoning Skills

Many young children have difficulty applying their reasoning skills when attempting to solve mathematics problems. In addition, children frequently struggle to put their thoughts into words as they attempt to communicate the logic behind their solution process in a manner that is convincing to others. Young children frequently do not explore their solution strategies in depth, because they tend to focus on finding the answer. As a result, young children often fail to realize that they can use their solution process to extend and expand their understanding of mathematics concepts.

## Capitalizing on Day-to-Day Events

To help young children overcome their inability to apply logic to the solution of problems, I have found that asking them to solve problems based on the day-to-day events and routines of the classroom are an effective way of fostering their reasoning abilities. Problems based on children's interactions with one another and their experiences with classroom materials are especially useful in helping beginning problem solvers see the connections between mathematics and the real world. In addition, classroom events and materials are familiar to, and seem to hold a special appeal for, young children.

## Encouraging Peer Sharing through Small-Group Discussions

I have also found that young children's reasoning and communication skills are enhanced when they have the opportunity to share and compare their ideas with those of their peers through small-group discussions. Unlike whole-class discussions, small-group discussions present an opportunity that is more conducive to—

- using guided discovery for learning new mathematics content;

- encouraging children to think more deeply about the mathematics concepts and ideas represented in problems, and applying reason and logic when solving problems;

- providing a forum for children who may be unwilling to share their ideas in front of the entire class;

- promoting mentoring of younger or less capable children by older or more capable students; and

- assessing the processes that children use to solve problems—children's problem-solving skills, strategies, attitudes, levels of understanding, and abilities to cooperate and collaborate with others in a mutually beneficial manner.

## Fostering Understanding

During the small-group discussions described in this and the next chapter, I frequently ask probing or leading questions (1) to encourage children to clarify their explanations and use proper mathematical terminology and (2) to check the children's level of understanding. I also encourage children to use their informal mathematical understandings to construct algebraic and geometric relationships based on the mass, shape, and size of various blocks. As the discussions demonstrate, the children were not only able to construct the desired algebraic and geometric relationships but on several occasions were also able to correct their own mistakes and make unexpected discoveries.

As stated in the NCTM's *Principles and Standards for School Mathematics (Principles and Standards)*, "algebraic ideas should emerge and be investigated as students—

- ... look for and apply relationships between varying quantities to make predictions;

- make and explain generalizations that seem to always work in particular situations" (NCTM 2000, p. 159).

*Principles and Standards* goes on to say that children should "[a]nalyze the characteristics and properties of two- and three-dimensional geometric shapes and develop mathematical arguments about geometric relationships" as well as "[u]se visualization, spatial reasoning, and geometric modeling to solve problems" (NCTM 2000, p. 96).

# Characteristics of Budding Problem Solvers

Throughout the small-group discussions described in chapters 3 and 4, the children exhibit several interesting, noteworthy characteristics in addition to their mathematical abilities:

## *Patience, perseverance, and positive attitude*

First, the children display various attitudes and dispositions not typically found in traditional mathematics classrooms, including a sense of *patience, perseverance,* and a *positive attitude.* They exhibit these positive dispositions not because they are especially talented students, nor because I have chosen particular classroom episodes that reflect these characteristics. Rather, the children display these traits because of a concerted effort in our classroom to develop them in all children. Both I and the older students model these behaviors for the younger children, and I constantly recognize children who display these characteristics. Over time, these attitudes are quite possibly the most important and universal problem-solving strategies that children can possess—they serve children well not only when solving problems in mathematics but also when overcoming difficulties and facing new challenges in life.

## *View of themselves as sense makers*

Second, the children see themselves as *sense makers,* and they expect mathematics to make sense. They approach problem solving as a sense-making activity as they craft their personal solutions to problems so that their solutions will make sense to others.

## *Eagerness to share solutions*

Third, the children are eager to share their solutions with one another. They have an expectation that after solving each problem, they will explain their solution to others and comment on the solution processes of their classmates.

## *A sense of community*

Fourth, the children display a sense of community. They show an interest in one another and try to help one another understand the mathematical concepts involved in the problems. Building a community of learners is perhaps one of the greatest challenges facing teachers, for the reason that young children tend to be self-centered and more interested in what they have to say than in what others have to share. This tendency is unfortunate because as the cartoon at the right points out, we all have much to learn from one another.

## Willingness to adopt or adapt strategies

Fifth, the children use what they know as a starting point for developing problem-solving strategies, and then fine-tune, modify, or adapt their individual strategies when faced with new challenges. During the course of the following activities, some of the children demonstrate a willingness to adopt a new strategy if their initial strategy proves unsuccessful. However, most of the children seem to prefer to modify an incorrect strategy as they attempt to make *their strategy* work.

"Dolly won't learn ANYTHING if she does all the talking."

"How come PJ got four sandwiches and I only got two?"

# Young Children's Thinking Patterns

Throughout the following chapters, many of the children's comments and solutions to the problems may come as a surprise to the reader, and their comments often remind me of the cartoon at the left.

I am constantly amazed by what young children say and do, and I have become convinced that in many ways, young children simply *do not think like adults.* That observation may seem obvious to anyone who has worked with young children. Yet when planning instructional units or selecting classroom activities, teachers often seem to ignore that fact and proceed in ways that treat children as if they think in ways similar to adults. Some of the major differences that I have observed in the thinking of young children and adults include nonlogical thinking, innocence and innovation, and circular logic.

## Nonlogical thinking

Adults may at times think illogically when solving problems, but young children seem to think nonlogically. Rather than use reason, young children frequently rely on past experiences or their senses to formulate hypotheses about events. This tendency often leads to false conclusions and to comments that adults find hard to understand.

## Innocence and innovation

Children display an innocence that allows them to craft truly creative and innovative solutions to problems. More than once, I have been challenged to understand what children are trying to say or do, because their solutions are either extremely unusual or represent unique ways of thinking about problems.

## Circular logic

When children do use a form of logic, it is usually not the type of linear logic used by adults (i.e., if $A = B$ and $B = C$, then $A = C$). Instead children use what has been characterized as *circular logic* (Piaget 1954). Jean Piaget was the first to observe and document children's use of circular logic. The following is an example of the use of circular logic that took place one day during a discussion between myself and a child.

| | |
|---|---|
| *Mr. B.:* | How did you solve the problem? |
| *Child:* | I did it in my head. |
| *Mr. B.:* | But what did you do in your head? |
| *Child:* | I solved the problem. |
| *Mr. B.:* | But how did you know your answer was correct? |
| *Child:* | Because the way I did it worked. |
| *Mr. B.:* | But how did you know the way you did it worked? |
| *Child:* | Because I got the answer. |

The reader will encounter another example of circular logic later in this chapter.

# Discussion Group 1

The descriptions of the discussion groups that appear in chapters 3 and 4 include some introductory remarks and unedited transcripts of the dialog that took place between the children and me. Interspersed throughout the transcripts of the discussions, I have also included commentaries to help the reader more fully understand the activities, my actions, and the actions of the children.

## Group 1's Problem

Two glue sticks balance block C. How many glue sticks do you predict will balance each of the other blocks on the table (fig. 3.1)?

(Note: Although only one set of Unit Blocks is shown in fig. 3.1, the actual classroom table contained several sets of Unit Blocks to give each child ready access to all the blocks.)

While I worked with the four children in the discussion group, the other twenty-seven children in the classroom (a) continued their personal investigations of the balance, (b) solved problems I had created on the basis of their investigations, or (c) authored their own problems for one another to solve.

The four children participating in the discussion group under consideration sat in pairs on opposite sides of a table. The table contained several sets of Unit Blocks. In the center of the table was a balance on which Unit Block C was balanced by two glue sticks. In addition, each child was given a copy of the recoding sheet in figure 3.2 to document information about the blocks used during the activity.

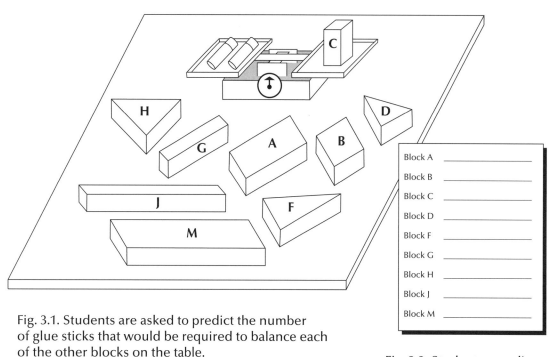

Fig. 3.1. Students are asked to predict the number of glue sticks that would be required to balance each of the other blocks on the table.

Fig. 3.2. Student recording sheet for the block-weighing activity

One pair of children included Nicholas, a first grader having average mathematical abilities, and his partner, Nicole, a second grader performing below grade level in mathematics. The other pair consisted of Melissa, a first grader having average mathematical abilities, and her partner, Taylor, a second-grade ESL student performing below grade level in mathematics. I frequently have children work with partners so that they can build their thinking on each other's ideas and practice using mathematical terminology.

## The Warm-Up

I began the discussion by asking the children some warm-up questions about the shapes on the table. As mentioned in the preceding chapter, I begin each problem-solving lesson with a short warm-up activity to introduce the lesson and give the children direct skills instruction. I have found that skills instruction is more effective when it is incorporated into problem-solving activities rather than presented to children as isolated drill-and-practice exercises. This particular warm-up activity helped to familiarize the children with the blocks on the table and the mathematical terms we would use throughout the activity.

As I picked up block B (fig. 3.1) off the table, I held it so that the square face of the block was facing toward the children as I began the discussion with a question.

| | |
|---|---|
| *Mr. B.:* | What shape is this face on the block? |
| *Nicole:* | What do you mean? |
| *Mr. B.:* | I'm not sure what you are asking? |
| *Nicole:* | What does *face* mean? |
| *Mr. B.:* | *Face* is what mathematicians call the flat surface on a block. What shape is this face on the block? |
| *Nicole:* | Oh, I get it. It's a square. |
| *Mr. B.:* | How do you know it is a square? |
| *Nicole.:* | Because it looks like a square. |
| *Mr. B.:* | But what does a square look like? |
| *Taylor:* | It has four sides. |
| *Mr. B.:* | What do you mean, "four sides"? [As I asked this question, Taylor pointed to the four edges on the square face of block B.] I'm still a little confused about what a square looks like, because a rectangle has four sides, but a rectangle is not a square. [As I made this statement, I rotated block B so that one of the rectangular faces was facing toward the children.] |
| *Taylor:* | The sides are not the same, but in a square they're the same. |
| *Mr. B.:* | What do you mean when you say the sides are "the same" in a square? |
| *Taylor:* | They are the same, like equal, like, if one side is 2, the rest are 2. |
| *Mr. B.:* | I'm still not sure what you mean? |
| *Nicholas:* | He means they are the same long |

| | |
|---|---|
| *Taylor:* | They are the same length, like, if one side is 2 inches, they are all 2 inches. |
| *Mr. B.:* | I agree that a square has four sides that are the same length. Is there anything else about a square that is the same?" |

The children seemed confused by this question, and a long pause ensued. After a while, Nicole ventured a response.

| | |
|---|---|
| *Nicole:* | I think they got four corners that are the same. |
| *Mr. B.:* | So how do you know when the shape is a square and when it is a rectangle? |
| *Nicholas:* | I think the square, they are the same, and the rectangle, the sides are different. |
| *Taylor:* | Yeah, like the square, they are all 2 inches, and the rectangle, they are 2 inches and 4 inches. |
| *Mr. B.:* | What is 2 inches and 4 inches? |
| *Taylor:* | Like, you take a square, and you stretch it out so two sides are longer than the other sides. |
| *Mr. B.:* | Now, I would like all of you to pick up one block B off the table, count the number of square faces, then count the number of rectangular faces, and write down your answers on your recording sheet. |

When the children were finished, we resumed our discussion.

| | |
|---|---|
| *Melissa:* | It's two squares and four rectangles. |
| *Mr. B.:* | I agree, so how many faces does block B have in all? |
| *Nicholas:* | Five (be)cause you count them: one, two, three, four, five [pointing to the faces on block B that he could "see" but failing to count the face that he could not see, which was flush against the table]. |
| *Melissa:* | I disagree because you didn't count the other one. [Nicholas seemed confused, so Melissa continued.] You got to pick it up so you can count the other one underneath. |
| *Nicholas:* | [Picking up the block and flashing a big smile] Oh, yeah, it is six, I agree with Melissa. |
| *Taylor:* | I agree, it's six because 2 + 4 = 6." |
| *Mr. B.:* | Why did you add 2 + 4? |

> *Taylor:* Because two square sides plus four rectangle sides is six sides.
>
> *Nicole:* I disagree because you called them *sides*, and they are faces; the block has two square faces and four rectangle faces, not sides.
>
> *Taylor:* I agree with Nicole.

Next I held up block D (fig. 3.1) with the triangular face toward the children, and continued with another question.

> *Mr. B:* What shape is this face?
>
> *Nicholas:* A triangle.
>
> *Mr. B.:* How do you know it is a triangle?
>
> *Nicole:* Because it has three sides.
>
> *Mr. B.:* What else does it have?
>
> *Nicole:* Three corners.
>
> *Mr. B.:* Pick up one block D off the table, count the number of triangle faces and rectangle faces, and write down your answers on your recording sheet.

When the children were finished recording, I asked Nicholas to share first.

> *Nicholas:* What I wrote is two triangles and three rectangles because this time I counted the one on the bottom and it's five.
>
> *Mr. B.:* I agree, and you even answered my next question. I was going to ask how many faces does block D have in all, but Nicholas already said five faces. Now I would like you to pick up one block A (fig. 3.1) off the table and count the number of rectangle faces that you see.

After the children were done examining the block, we resumed our discussion.

> *Melissa:* I think it's four.
>
> *Taylor:* I disagree because it's six.
>
> *Nicholas:* I agree with Melissa, it's four (be)cause, look, it's "one, two, three, four" [pointing to the four small faces on block A as indicated in figure 3.3].
>
> *Taylor:* You didn't count the other ones.

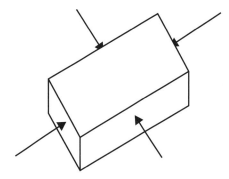

Fig. 3.3. Nicholas counted "one, two, three, four" as he pointed to the indicated faces on block A.

*Melissa:* Yes he did, he counted them all.

*Taylor:* But the ones on the top and bottom are rectangles, too [picking up block A and holding it so one of the large rectangular faces was facing toward Nicholas and Melissa as he continued]. What shape is this?

*Nicholas:* I don't know.

*Taylor:* It's a rectangle just like the other ones.

*Melissa:* No, it's not skinny like the other ones.

*Taylor:* But it is a fat rectangle.

*Mr. B.:* I think Taylor is saying that not all rectangles look the same. Some are skinny, like Melissa said, but some are wider, like Taylor said.

At this point I drew several four-sided shapes on a piece of paper (fig.3.4) and had the children take turns identifying which shapes are rectangles and which are not.

Fig. 3.4. Teacher-drawn four-sided shapes among which the children were asked to identify the rectangles

## The Children's Language

Although the answers to some of the questions I posed in the preceding warm-up activity may seem obvious to the reader, they were not obvious to the children, as revealed by their comments. From the children's perspective, learning the language of *school mathematics* may seem somewhat like learning a second language, because many children are rarely exposed to mathematical terms outside of school. For that reason teachers need to offer students an enriched environment that gives them the time and experiences they need to gradually acquire mathematical vocabularies.

Most young children enter school with a very small mathematical vocabulary that is often limited to such terms as *equal, plus, take away, square, circle,* and *triangle.* But even those terms have vague meanings for children, and children often use them in ways that are not mathematically correct. For example, some of the children in the preceding discussion had difficulty recognizing rectangles that were not like the "skinny ones" they had previously seen. Researchers have found that young children have similar difficulty recognizing triangles that do not look like equilateral triangles (Clements and Sarama 2000; Hannibal 1999). Children also have misconceptions about basic mathematical symbols. Several researchers have found that many children think the equals sign means "the answer comes next" rather than indicates equivalency (Baroody and Ginsburg 1983; Falkner, Levi, and Carpenter 1999; Saenz-Ludlow and Walgamuth 1998). As an example, when children were asked what number goes in the box for the number sentence in figure 3.5, they usually answered 7.

$$2 \; + \; 5 \; = \; \boxed{\phantom{0}} \; + \; 3$$

Fig. 3.5. Children are shown this number sentence and are asked what number goes in the box.

Research into language acquisition has shown that before children can use words in their speaking vocabularies, they must first add those words to their listening vocabularies. Likewise, children must first add words to their speaking vocabularies before they can use those words meaningfully in their writing vocabularies. All these processes take time and require numerous opportunities to practice using words in meaningful contexts.

In addition to helping children expand their mathematical vocabularies, warm-up activities accomplish other important goals: (1) they give teachers a forum for direct skills instruction, as well as an opportunity to model asking clarifying questions, and (2) they give children a chance to practice mental mathematics skills and to fine-tune their communication skills.

## The Problem-Solving Segment of the Lesson

Having completed the warm-up part of the lesson, I began the problem-solving portion of the lesson.

> *Mr. B.:*   The other day I noticed that Melissa and Taylor discovered that two glue sticks balance block C (fig. 3.1). I have repeated their experiment with the balance on the table, and you can see that Melissa and Taylor were correct. Today I am going to ask you to think like a mathematician. You are going to use Melissa's and Taylor's discovery along with what mathematicians call *reasoning* to solve some problems and make some predictions. After you have made each prediction, share with your partner how you solved the problem, and then have your partner tell you why she or he agrees or disagrees with what you have done. When everyone is finished sharing with their partner, you can explain how you solved the problem to the whole group, and we will comment on your solution or ask you questions. Here is your first problem:
>
> If two glue sticks balance block C, how many glue sticks do you predict will balance block B (fig. 3.1)?
>
> [As I posed this problem and all subsequent problems, I held up samples of the blocks so that the children could easily locate them on the table.]

Taylor began to compare block C with block B, and seemed to have concluded that the size of the block was related to its weight. The other three children appeared confused and unsure of what the problem was asking them to do.

> *Melissa:*   [Immediately trying to take block C off the balance and replace it with block B] Can I change the blocks on the balance and see its weight?

30

> *Mr. B.:* Today I would like you to make your predictions using what you know about the block on the balance—block C—and what you know about the other blocks on the table.
>
> *Melissa:* But can't I just put this one (block B) on and weigh it?
>
> *Mr. B.:* Today I would like you to think about what the weight might be— what would make sense. Try to make a prediction about the weight of the block using what you already know.

## *Recording predictions*

Melissa grudgingly agreed not to use the balance and instead picked up one block C in her right hand and one block B in her left hand. Then she moved her hands up and down in the air like a balance as she compared the weight of the two blocks. When she was finished using her *hand balance,* she wrote her estimate for the weight of block B on her paper.

> *Taylor:* I think I got it, it's four.
>
> *Mr. B.:* When you think you know the answer to the problem, write it on your paper and then wait to share your answer when everyone is ready. When you say the answer out loud, it robs others of the opportunity to make their own discoveries, and it disrupts their thinking.
>
> *Taylor:* OK, I'll write it down; it's four.

After the children had recorded their predictions, they shared their thinking with their partner. Melissa was first to share her solution with the whole group.

> *Melissa:* [Demonstrating how she estimated the weight of block B using her hands] It's about three glue sticks because I can tell this one (block B) is a little more weight. So I think it is three, but I don't really know.
>
> *Mr. B.:* That is a good estimate, but did anyone solve the problem in a way that you can be sure your prediction is accurate?
>
> *Nicholas:* I think two.
>
> *Mr. B.:* Why do you think two glue sticks will balance block B?
>
> *Nicholas:* How I figured it out. I went "one glue stick, two glue stick" [pointing to the two block Cs that he had placed on top of block B, as shown in figure 3.6, and counting them].

I was just about to ask Nicholas some *probing questions* to more fully understand his solution strategy, which appeared to be correct. I suspected that he had arrived at the wrong answer because he had counted by ones instead of twos—two glue sticks equal the weight of one block C. However, before I could ask Nicholas any questions, he removed both block Cs from block B and laid his pen across block B. He pretended to "cut" block B into three pieces.

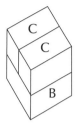

Fig. 3.6. Nicholas stacked two block Cs on top of one block B to demonstrate his solution.

*Nicholas:* No, wait, I went "one glue stick, two glue stick, three glue stick" [demonstrating his "cuts" as shown in figure 3.7].

*Nicole:* I agree (be)cause that's how I did it. I think it is three glue sticks.

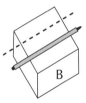

Fig. 3.7. Nicholas demonstrates his "cuts" of block B to support his solution.

## Dealing with an incorrect response

When children give an incorrect response, I always find it hard to tell whether the difficulty they are having lies with the language or the mathematical aspects of the problem—much like the clerk in the cartoon on the following page. In this particular situation, I wondered whether Nicholas's lack of understanding of the problem was due to the way it was worded or to his inability to apply the mathematical concepts necessary to solve the problem correctly.

*Mr. B.:* I think I understand what you are saying, but I'm a little confused. Nicholas, when you "cut" block B into pieces, how do you know the pieces are the same as one glue stick?

> *Nicholas:* I just know (be)cause when you cut it, you get three glue sticks, not two like I said before, but I was wrong.
>
> *Melissa:* I agree because when I weighed it with my hands, it was three, and so when you cut it (block B), it is three glue sticks like Nicholas said. So I agree, we are right.
>
> *Taylor:* I disagree (be)cause it's four glue sticks. Like Nicholas almost had it (be)cause, look, two of these (block C) is the same as this one (block B) [placing two block Cs on top of block B in the way that Nicholas had previously done, as shown in figure 3.6]. And this block (one block C on top of block B) is the same as this one (block C on the balance), and this block (the other block C on top of block B) is the same as this one (block C on the balance). So it's 2 + 2 is 4. So I think it is four glue sticks because these two (two block Cs) are the same as this one (block B).
>
> *Nicole:* Now I agree with Taylor. I think it is four like he said.

## Employing lending questions

I suspected that the other children did not fully grasp the reasoning behind Taylor's solution, and so I attempted to help them understand Taylor's logic by asking some *leading questions.* As I held up one of the block Cs, I asked, "How many glue sticks will balance this small rectangular block C?" Nicole and Nicholas both replied, "Two." I then picked up another block C and repeated the question. Again both Nicholas and Nicole said, "Two." Then I placed the two block Cs side by side on the table and asked, "How many glue sticks would it take to balance both block Cs altogether?" Nicole thought about this question for a long time and then very tentatively answered, "Four." Meanwhile, Nicholas had picked up his pen and proceeded to "cut" the two block Cs into three glue sticks in the same manner as he had divided block B.

The reader may be puzzled by these children's difficulty in seeing something that to an adult is quite obvious. Children can be tantalizingly close to understanding an idea, yet at the

same time be very far away from fully comprehending what others are trying to say, as in the cartoon above. For children to make this kind of leap in understanding, they must first abandon their current way of thinking and then "see" the solution to the problem in an entirely new way. That process is very difficult for children because they must construct their new understanding on their own—someone else cannot do it for them.

I repeated the foregoing process using two block Cs. Young children, like Nicholas, will usually not abandon their current way of thinking without seeing a different solution several times, and sometimes over several days. Children have a tendency to hang onto an idea for lengths of time that may appear unreasonable to an adult. Also, some children, like Nicole, need to see the solution a second time so they can verify their initial thinking. This time, both Nicholas and Nicole thought about the problem for a long time as they studied the two block Cs laid side by side.

## Stepping back versus stepping in

When children think about a problem for any length of time, the delay can create a feeling of tension in the group, and teachers often choose to intervene rather than let children solve the problem themselves. Teachers face a difficult dilemma in knowing when to *step in* versus when to *step back* so that children can do their own thinking.

Finally, Nicole excitedly said, "Oh, now I get it. It is four, like I said before. I agree with Taylor. That (one of the block Cs) equals 'one, two' and that (the other block C) equals 'one, two,' and so it's 'one, two, three, four.' So I agree, it is four glue sticks."

> *Nicholas:* I agree with Taylor, too, (be)cause it is four glue sticks.
>
> *Mr. B.:* So, help me understand what you are saying. If it takes four glue sticks to balance two block Cs, how many glue sticks does it take to balance one block B?"

Nicole took one block B and stood it upright on the table, and then she stood two block Cs on the top of block B, as shown in figure 3.8. Nicole looked at the blocks from all angles and said, "Yep, they are the same. It's four glue sticks like before."

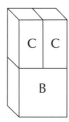

Fig. 3.8. Nicole's block arrangement to show that two block Cs
are equal to one block B

Nicholas very emphatically said, "Oh, I get it, I agree. This (the two block Cs) is four and this (he points to block B) is four (be)cause they are the same."

### Asking probing questions

At this point the reader might think that both Nicole and Nicholas have understood Taylor's solution to the problem, since they can state the correct answer and Nicole can model her thinking with the blocks. However, I have found that jumping to conclusions can be misleading when working with young children. Sometimes teachers need to take the time to explore children's thinking more deeply by asking probing questions, such as, "Why do you think that?" or "How did you figure it out?" Asking these kinds of questions can reveal children's misconceptions and can help teachers better assess children's current level of understanding.

> *Mr. B.:*   I can see how Nicole used the blocks to solve the problem, but Nicholas, I am unsure of how you know that it would take four glue sticks to balance block B. Nicholas, can you show me why you think the answer is four glue sticks.

Once again, Nicholas took his pen and "cut" block B into pieces as he said, "I cuts it in half, and then I cuts it in half again, so it is four glue sticks."

To the reader, Nicholas might appear to have been ignoring the information provided by the objects on the balance as well as the relationship between the size of the blocks and their weight. Although he did not seem to realize that block B is twice the size of block C (and therefore that block B is twice the weight of block C), he was using the information provided by the objects on the balance, but in an unusual way. He seemed to be trying to "cut" block B into pieces of wood that would be the same size as one glue stick. Nicholas was trying to make sense of the problem, but in a way that most adults might find questionable. As noted previously, young children's thought processes are often very different from those of adults.

Nicholas appeared to be using a type of personal logic that made sense to him but was very difficult for others to understand.

When children use this type of personal logic, it can create a situation that is confusing for both the teacher and the other children in the discussion group, especially if those children are capable of using more sophisticated forms of thinking. Realizing the Nicholas had arrived at the right answer of four glue sticks using a questionable strategy, I was about to ask some more questions, but before I could ask my first question, Nicole made the following comment.

> *Nicole:* I agree they (Taylor and Nicholas) both got the answer, but I agree with how Nicholas did it because he cut the block into the glue sticks and counted them.
>
> *Melissa:* I agree with Nicole. Nicholas's way works a lot better than Taylor's.
>
> *Taylor:* I agree with Nicholas, because you can cut it into four glue sticks like he said.

An interesting observation at this point is that all the children seemed to think that Nicholas's solution was more reasonable than Taylor's—even though Taylor had clearly solved the problem in the manner that most adults would find logical. Sometimes when such an outcome occurs, I sense that I am the "odd one out" in the group, and from the children's perspective, I am the one who does not understand how to solve the problem. This feeling can be very uncomfortable for the teacher, and teachers can be tempted to correct the situation by simply explaining to children the *adult* way of solving the problem. However, I decided to ask some more questions.

> *Mr. B.:* How is the square block B like the two block Cs?
>
> *Taylor:* They are the same.
>
> *Mr. B.:* Taylor, what do you mean. "They are the same"?
>
> *Taylor:* They are the same size, like when I put them (the two block Cs) like this (on top of block B), they are the same. See, you can see it; they match up.
>
> *Nicole:* I agree with Taylor (be)cause when I stand them up, they are kind of, like, the same shape, only one is split in half (the two block Cs).
>
> *Mr. B.:* I agree they are the same shape, but are they the same size?
>
> *Taylor:* Yes, because if you take this (one block C) and this (another block C) and put them together, and they make this square block. And if you put them like this [Taylor placed both block Cs on top of block B], they match up, and if you put them like this [Taylor placed both

> block Cs on the table beside block B], they match up how thick they are.
>
> *Nicholas:* Oh now, I get it. They gots to be the same, so they weigh the same.
>
> *Mr. B.:* Nicholas, what has to be the same?
>
> *Nicholas:* The blocks, like they got to match to weigh the same.

## Allowing for observation and reflection

Although I am not entirely convinced that Nicholas actually "gets it," I decided to present the next problem to the children. At this point the reader may be wondering what had happened to Melissa. Neither I nor her classmates were ignoring Melisssa, rather we were simply giving her the chance to listen and observe what the others had to say about the blocks. If Melissa had not been engaged in the activity, I would have attempted to draw her attention to our discussion. However, I could see that she was carefully watching what the other children were doing and was intently listening to what the other children were saying. I suspected that she was thinking very hard about the questions being discussed, but that she may have been confused about what the activity required her to do. Some teachers think that they must constantly involve all children in discussions, when in fact some children need time just to observe and reflect on the actions of others before they feel confident enough to participate in discussions themselves.

> *Mr. B.:* Here is your next problem. If two glue sticks balance block C, how many glue sticks do you predict will balance block G (fig. 3.1)?

This time all the children immediately began to explore a solution to the problem using the blocks on the table, and as will be revealed by the following discussion, they all developed uniquely different solution strategies.

I have always been intrigued by the way children approach the solution to a problem as compared with the way they approach drill-and-practice exercises. Although these children were sitting next to one another at the table, they seemed unaware of what the others were doing. Sense making would appear to be a very personal activity that requires a high degree of concentration. This level of engagement is in sharp contrast with the behaviors that children sometimes exhibit when completing worksheets, for example, straying off task or copying answers from one another, as in the cartoon on the next page.

Seemingly, when the goal of an activity is different, then the means for achieving the goal can also be very different. Most children quickly realize that the goal of most worksheets is to get it done as quickly as possible. However, when the goal is sense making, children exhibit markedly different behaviors as they attempt to craft personal solutions to problems so that their solutions make sense to themselves and, they hope, to others as well.

After all the children had recorded their estimates and shared their solutions with their partners, we resumed our discussion as I requested, "Nicole will you share first?"

## Sharing solutions

Nicole arranged the blocks as shown in figure 3.9 by standing block G upright and then placing both block Cs end-to-end on top of block G. She then said, "Yep, they're the same." Next she placed both block Cs end-to-end beside block G, as shown in figure 3.10, and once again commented, "Yep, they're still the same." Interestingly, about 25 percent of the children in the class solved the problems by standing the blocks upright (using a vertical orientation) rather than laying the blocks flat on the table in a horizontal position.

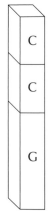

Fig. 3.9. Nicole's first vertical block arrangement to demonstrate that two block Cs are the same size as one block G

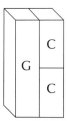

Fig. 3.10. Nicole's second vertical block arrangement to demonstrate that two block Cs are the same size as one block G

> *Nicole:*  What I did is, I think it is four glue sticks (be)cause I said, well, this one (block C) is "one, two" glue sticks (be)cause we already know that, and this one (the other block C) is "one, two" glue sticks (be)cause we already know that, so this one is "one, two, three, four" glue sticks (be)cause "one, two" and "one, two" is four.

> *Taylor:* Why did you count by ones—you could have counted by twos and it's easier.

Nicole did not seem to understand Taylor's comment, so I asked Nicole if she could count by twos, and she replied that she could. I next asked her how many glue sticks would balance block C, and she answered, "Two." I then asked her how many glue sticks would balance two block Cs, and she counted by ones to four.

## Introducing a Minilesson

I therefore decided to do a minilesson on counting by twos, during which I attempted to show how that way of counting could be used as a tool to make solving some problems more efficient. By pursuing problem-solving activities in which new skills are embedded, children are given the chance to practice and apply skills in a meaningful context. Too often children practice skills in isolation from a context in which the skill can serve as a useful tool. Drill and practice does help children become more efficient in the use of skills, but children learn how to effectively apply skills in problem-solving situations. Giving children the opportunity to apply skills within a meaningful context also helps to answer the question frequently asked by children, "Why do I need to learn this?"

After our minilesson on counting by twos was finished, I resumed our discussion by returning to Nicole's solution to the problem.

> *Mr. B.:* Nicole, how did you know that block G is the same as the two block Cs?
>
> *Nicole:* Well, when I put them like this [arranges the blocks as in figure 3.10]. I could see that they are the same.
>
> *Mr. B.:* How are they the same?
>
> *Nicole:* Well, when I measure like this, they are the same.

Nicole arranged the blocks as in figure 3.9. She then used her hands to "measure" the length of the two block Cs placed end to end, and then moved her hands down to compare this measurement with the length of block G. She then rearranged the blocks as in figure 3.10. Once again she used her hands as a measuring tool, but this time she measured the width of one of the block Cs and compared it with the width of block G. This approach struck me as rather odd because using figure 3.9 would seem more appropriate to compare the width of the blocks (rather than the length), and using figure 3.10 would seem more appropriate to compare the length of the blocks (rather than the width). Nicole, however, chose to use the two arrangements of the blocks in a decidedly different manner. Sometimes I find that children's logic, such as Nicole's way of solving this problem, is difficult to understand. But I always find children's logic interesting and sometimes humorous, as in the following cartoon.

*Taylor:* I agree because it's just like before, only I went like this [arranges the blocks as in figure 3.11]. And it's just like the last time, only you put them (the two block Cs) a different way, so it's 2 + 2 = 4.

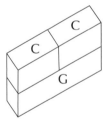

Fig. 3.11. Taylor's different arrangement of the two block Cs in relationship to block G

*Nicholas:* But how did you know they are the same?

*Taylor:* I match them up just like I did the last time. See, they are the same. So the glue sticks is the same. Four glue sticks here (two block Cs) and four glue sticks here (block G).

*Nicholas:* Well, I agree it's four.

*Mr. B.:* How do you know the answer is four?

*Nicholas:* Well, I did it kind of different. What I did is, I put them like this [arranges the blocks as in figure 3.12], and I said that this (block C) is two glue sticks [placing his pen on block C and "cutting" it in half (into two glue sticks)] and this (the other block C) is two glue sticks [again placing his pen on the other block C and "cutting" it in half]. So it's got to be four glue sticks if you glue them (two block Cs) together to make this one (block G).

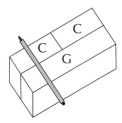

Fig. 3.12. Nicholas made this arrangement and demonstrated "cuts" with his pen.

*Melissa:* I agree (be)cause I did it like this [positioning the blocks as in figure 3.13], and I counted them (four block Cs) like this, "One, two, three, four," so I think it is four.

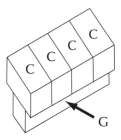

Fig. 3.13. Melissa's block arrangement to demonstrate her strategy

At this point Nicole and Taylor seemed puzzled by what Nicholas and Melissa had done. On the one hand, they could see that both Nicholas and Melissa had gotten the correct answer, but on the other hand, they were not sure about the two solution strategies.

This behavior is very typical of young children. When one of their peers gets the correct answer but has used an unusual strategy or one that contains an error in logic, children often do not quite know what to say—after all, if the answer is right, maybe the strategy is correct also. I could have intervened and attempted to guide the discussion, but I chose not to say anything and waited to see what the children would do. After a long pause, Taylor began to speak.

*Taylor:*  I agree and disagree. Like, I agree she got the answer, but how did you do it?

*Melissa:*  I counted them up, one, two, three, four (the four block Cs). So I think it is four.

*Taylor:*  I agree that it cuts it into four glue sticks, but you can't do it that way.

*Mr. B.:*  Why don't you think Melissa's way makes sense?

*Taylor:*  They aren't the same.

*Mr. B.:*  What do you mean, "They aren't the same"?

*Taylor:*  [Lifting the four C blocks off of block G and laying them beside block G as in figure 3.14] See, these (four block Cs) are not the same size as this one (block G).

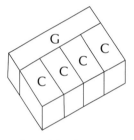

Fig. 3.14. Taylor's block arrangement to demonstrate that four block Cs are not the same size as one block G

*Melissa*
*and*
*Nicholas:*  Yes they are.

*Mr. B.:*  How are they the same?

*Nicholas:*  They are the same long.

*Melissa:*  I agree with Nicholas, they are the same long.

*Taylor:*  But they don't make the same shape. It takes two of these (block G) to make these blocks (four block Cs) [taking two G blocks and placing them on top of the four block Cs]. See, it would take two, four, six, eight glue sticks to balance those blocks (four block Cs), not four.

*Nicole:*  I agree with Taylor. They (four block Cs) don't make the same shape,

> so they don't weigh the same (be)cause, look, they are hanging over on both sides [placing the four block Cs back on top of block G as in figure 3.13].
>
> *Nicholas:* I agree with Nicole, they don't match up, but they do cut it into four pieces, so I kinda still agree she got it.
>
> *Taylor:* But her way doesn't work. Like it works (be)cause she gets the answer, but you can't put them (four block Cs) like that because like Nicole says, they won't match up.

## Taking a Break for Reflection

> *Mr. B.:* I agree with Taylor and Nicole that in order for the blocks to balance, they have to be the same size, and one way to check to see if they are the same size is to see if they are the same shape. All of you have done some excellent thinking this morning, but it is time to take a break. Keep thinking about the problems you have solved, and we will solve some more problems later on.

Rather than complete an entire activity, I often give children a chance to do something different and then continue the activity at a later time. We reconvened the group later in the day and resumed our discussion.

> *Mr. B.:* You know that two glue sticks balance block C, and this morning you predicted that four glue sticks balance block B and [block] G. How many glue sticks will balance block A (fig. 3.1)?

As before, all four children used different solution strategies, but this time they took far less time to solve the problem. After the children recorded their answers and shared their solutions with their partners, I called on Nicholas to explain how he had solved the problem.

> *Nicholas:* I cuts it like this [placing his pen as shown in figure 3.15], and then I cut it again [moving his pen over one block], and then I cut it again [moving his pen over another block], and then I counted "one, two, three, four," but it's not four (be)cause they are each two, so it's twice as much, so I think it is eight glue sticks to make it balance.

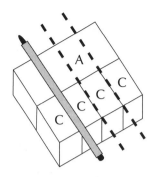

Fig. 3.15. Nicholas's block arrangement demonstrating that four block Cs, or eight glue sticks, are needed to balance block A

*Melissa:*   I disagree. I did it like this [arranges the blocks as in figure 3.16]. And you count them, and it is four.

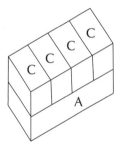

Fig. 3.16. Melissa's block arrangement to demonstrate an answer different from Nicholas's

*Nicholas:* But Melissa, it's not counting by ones, it's counting by twos (be)cause this one (block C) is two glue sticks and this one (block C) is two glue sticks and this one (block C) is two glue sticks and this one (block C) is two glue sticks. So it's "two, four, six, eight" glue sticks.

*Taylor:*   I agree with Nicholas because I did it two ways and got the same thing both times. First I did it this way [arranging the blocks as in figure 3.17], and it's eight glue sticks because this one (block G) cuts it (block A) in half [placing one block G on top of block A and then sliding block G across block A, showing that in either position it divides block A in half]. So it's 4 + 4 is 8.

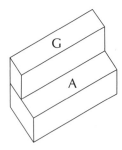

Fig. 3.17. Taylor's first arrangement to demonstrate
his agreement with Nicholas's answer

> *Taylor:* Then I did it this way [arranges the blocks as in figure 3.18], and it's
> eight glue sticks because 4 + 4 is 8. You just cut this one (block A)
> a different way. The first way, you cut it the length way, and you get
> two of these (block G). The next way, you cut it (block A) the other
> way, and you get two of the block Bs [as before, modeling how block
> B "cuts" block A in half by sliding block B back and forth across the
> surface of block A]. So I think it is eight glue sticks.

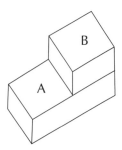

Fig. 3.18. Taylor's second arrangement demonstrating
his agreement with Nicholas's answer

## The Emergence of Abstract Thinking

At this point the reader should note that Taylor used some blocks other than block C to solve
this problem. This approach may seem like a minor step in thinking about the relationships
among the various blocks, but in fact it represents a major step that is difficult for many children
to make during the course of a single activity. Most children are such *literal* thinkers that they
can solve these problems only by comparing blocks with the block on the scale (block C).
However, Taylor showed that he could think more *abstractly* about the blocks, using what he
knew about each block to serve as a reference point for solving problems in an entirely new way.

> *Nicole:* I agree with Taylor (be)cause it is eight glue sticks, because I did it
> a different way and I got the same thing, so I think it is eight glue

sticks. How I did it was, I went, well, these are the same, and "one, two, three, four" [starting to count the block Cs by ones but then pausing and looking at Taylor]. No, wait, it's this way; 2 + 2 + 2 + 2 does equal 8 [first standing one block A on its side and placing four block Cs next to one end as in figure 3.19, then using her hands to once again measure the length of block A and comparing this measurement with the length of two block Cs]. Next I did it this way, and these are the same, and 2 + 2 + 2 + 2 + is 8 [moving the four block Cs and placing them in front of block A as in figure 3.20, once again using her hands to compare the height of block A and the height of two block Cs].

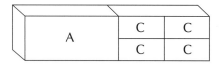

Fig. 3.19. Nicole's first arrangement to demonstrate agreement with Taylor's answer

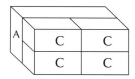

Fig. 3.20. Nicole's second arrangement to demonstrate agreement with Taylor's answer

*Taylor:*   Why did you measure them with your hands?" You can see they are the same.

*Nicole:*   I wanted to be sure.

*Melissa:*   I agree with Nicole, it is eight because she measured them to be sure.

*Mr. B.:*   All of you are doing some great problem solving, so here is your next problem. You know that two glue sticks balance block C. How many glue sticks do you predict will balance block D (fig. 3.1)?

## Approaching Challenging Problems

From past experiences, I knew that this problem would be the most challenging one for the children to solve, primarily because it asked them to develop a strategy that was completely different from the strategies most of them had come to rely on during the course of the activity. When doing these kinds of activities, I usually place the most challenging problem next-to-last and then follow it with a less challenging problem. This tactic accomplishes two things. First, if the children cannot solve the most challenging problem, I can always say, "This must be a very good problem, so let's put it in the back of our brains and let our brains think about it for awhile." Second, it allows the children to finish the activity with a problem that ensures a higher degree of success so that they can leave the activity with a sense of accomplishment.

All the children attempted to predict the number of glue sticks that would balance block D by using the same strategies they had used with the previous problems.

Nicholas, tried to cut block D in half using his pen, as shown in figure 3.21, but decided that the two pieces "don't make any of them" (the other blocks on the table).

Fig. 3.21. Nicholas's attempt to "cut"
block D in half with his pen

*Nicholas:* This is hard.

*Mr. B.:* I agree, the most interesting problems are sometimes the most difficult to solve, but when you solve them, it makes you feel very good inside because you know that what you did was special.

Nicole tried standing bock D upright and measuring it with her hands, but she became frustrated with this method. She then tried to "make" block D by outlining it with some of the other blocks. Surprisingly, a number of children in the classroom also attempted to use this *enclosure* method, illustrated in figure 3.22, to solve this problem.

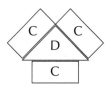

Fig. 3.22. Nicole's block arrangement, shown in front view for clarity: one block C rests on the table, one block D stands upright on top of it, and two block Cs rest atop block D, held in place by the student so they do not slide off.

Taylor first placed block C on top of block D, then removed block C and placed block B on top of block D, and finally removed block B and placed block A on top of block D. Next Taylor tried placing block D on top of each of the other blocks on the table. Finally he placed block C back on top of block D, as shown in figure 3.23. According to Taylor, the three corners on block D equal one glue stick, and the rest of block D equals two glue sticks because it is "close" to the size of block C.

Fig. 3.23. The blocks in Taylor's arrangement, shown from above:
block D is placed flat on the table, and block C rests on top of it.

*Taylor:*　I don't really know, but I think the corners sticking out of this one (block D) are probably about one glue stick. I'm not sure. I'm just estimating that the corners weigh one glue stick, and the rest is the same as this one (block C), so it's 2 + 1 = 3 glue sticks.

*Nicole:*　I disagree because if you cut off the corners, it's not a triangle any more, it's not the shape we're trying to find.

*Taylor:*　I know, but I put them (the corners) back on, and that's why it's one more glue stick, not the two glue sticks like the one (block C) on the balance.

None of the children seemed to notice that the corners of block C extended over block D until Nicholas finally resumed the discussion.

*Nicholas:*　Taylor, I agree and disagree, (be)cause the corners (block D) would be about one glue stick, but you haven't fitted all of this one (block C) on top of block D.

*Taylor:*　I know, but I can't make it fit like it is supposed to, so I just estimated that it was close.

## The complexity of a multistep process

Up to this point all the problems could be solved in a similar manner—block B is the same size as two block Cs, block G is the same size as two block Cs, and block A is the same size as four block Cs. In each instance the children could use a number of block Cs to "make" the shape of the other blocks. However, using block C does not directly lead to a solution of the problem involving block D.

Sometimes as adults we overlook the complexity of a solution to a problem and the number of steps required to arrive at an answer. As adults our minds can proceed through multiple steps so rapidly that they almost seem like a single action. To give the reader an idea of how difficult the problem involving block D is for young children, I have broken down the steps for the two ways that most children solve this problem.

The first approach often used by children is to join two block Ds to make a square. However, joining two block Ds in this way is very difficult for young children even when someone has shown them how to do it. Next, children must realize that the square shape they have made with the two block Ds is the same shape and size as one block B. Then children must remember, or once again determine, the number of glues sticks that will balance block B. Last, children must realize that two block Ds weigh the same as one block B, and therefore the weight of one block D is one-half the weight of block B.

The second approach used by young children is to realize that the problem can be solved using one block D and another block (usually block B, although a few children will use block A). To use this approach, however, children must engage in a truly different kind of thinking than the *adding up* or *counting* methods they have used with the other blocks in the activity. In contrast, this problem can be solved by observing that when block D is placed in just the right position on top of block B, it is one-half the size of block B. Children can then reason that because block D is one-half the size of block B, it is one-half the weight of block B, or two glue sticks.

Although the steps in each of the two solution processes just described may seem apparent to most adults, they are not at all apparent to many young children. Accomplishing each step in the multistep processes just described, however, is not what stands in the way of most children's attempts to solve this problem. A far more difficult roadblock for children is the necessity of using their brain in a manner that is not compatible with the way the brain likes to operate.

## The role of creativity

The brain is a pattern-seeking organ, and generally this trait is beneficial. Patterns help us make sense of things—they organize events, reveal relationships between objects, and lend a sense of predictability to our world. Without the ability to recognize patterns, learning would be extremely difficult because everything would appear as random events unrelated to one another. However, this tendency of the brain to search out patterns can sometimes cause difficulty for children when they need to think "outside the box," such as when they are engaged in problem-solving activities that require new ways of thinking.

Solving problems frequently requires a certain degree of creativity to move beyond a person's current way of thinking. Doing so is very difficult for young children, especially when their current pattern of thinking has helped them successfully solve previous problems. The role of creativity in solving problems is one way that problem solving significantly differs from doing drill-and-practice exercises. Traditional mathematics instruction has focused on helping children remember computation facts and algorithms. Children are taught that to use an algorithm successfully, the one thing that the solver does not want to do is think creatively. Computation algorithms work only when one thinks "inside the box"—when one follows each step of the algorithm precisely.

*"Never, ever, think outside the box."*

Of course, algorithms were created for precisely that reason—they provide a process that can be used with any numbers, and if the steps of the algorithm are followed exactly, they yield the correct answer every time. Similarly, the strategies that the children in the foregoing discussions had perfected were useful in finding the correct answers to several block-comparison problems, but now those same strategies interfered with their ability to solve the problem involving block D.

The block-D problem required someone who could think creatively—someone who could think outside the box, someone who had carefully observed the others in the group and listened to their comments, someone who had slowly gained confidence in herself and her abilities as a problem solver—someone like Melissa.

Over the years I have seen many children successfully determine the weight of block D using one of the two methods previously described. But I had never before seen the method used by Melissa. When Melissa first described her solution to the group, I was not sure whether she had truly solved the problem or had arrived at the correct answer through pure luck, because the solution method she used was the same strategy she had used with all the other problems. I would like to think that Melissa had a sudden insight based on her observations and the discussions that took place during this interview session. However, even now I am left with the uneasy feeling of not knowing whether her ingenious strategy for solving the block D problem represented a genuine leap in understanding or a timely coincidence in events. Melissa's solution is shown in figure 3.24.

Fig. 3.24. Melissa's arrangement, with block D laying flat on the table and block C resting on top of block D

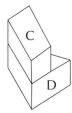 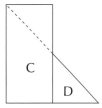

Fig. 3.24. Melissa's arrangement, with block D laying flat on the table and block C resting on top of block D

*Melissa:*    Well, I did it kinda like Taylor, but I think it is two glue sticks (be)cause they are both kinda like the same. But you have to cut off the corner of block D that is sticking out, kinda like Taylor did. But then you have to put it over here [pointing to the space under the corner of block C that was protruding over the edge of block D], and then the blocks would be the same. So they are both two glue sticks.

*Taylor:*    I disagree (be)cause block D is bigger than this one (block C), so it's got to weigh more like three glue sticks or something, and besides, you didn't make the shape.

*Mr. B.:*    Taylor, what do you mean when you say Melissa didn't make the shape?

*Taylor:*    She didn't make the triangle shape with the other blocks like we did before. She made the other block (block C), but that's not the one we are trying to figure out. She should have made this one (block D), not that one (block C).

*Nicholas:*    I agree with Taylor. This one (block D) is bigger, so it has to weigh more.

*Mr. B.:*    Nicholas and Taylor, how do you know block D is bigger than block C?

*Taylor:*    You just look at them and you can see.

*Nicholas:*    Yeah, you just look, and you can see the points sticking out, so it has to be bigger.

| | |
|---|---|
| *Nicole:* | Melissa, why do you think the piece you cut off will fit in the space underneath that block (block C)? |
| *Melissa:* | It just looks like it will fit in the space. |
| *Mr. B.:* | I think I might know a way to see if Melissa is correct. I would like everyone to get a piece of paper from the paper drawer and trace around both block C and block D. [Pause] Label your drawings block C and block D, and cut out both blocks. [Pause] Now, place the drawing of block C on top of the drawing of block D, just as Melissa has done with the blocks on the table, and draw a line on block D using the edge of block C so you know just how much to cut off. [Pause] Cut off the corner of block D, and move it over to see if the two pieces make the same shape as block C. |

The children followed the directions, and when they were done, we resumed our discussion of Melissa's solution to the problem.

| | |
|---|---|
| *Nicole:* | It works—they are the same, just like she thought. |
| *Taylor:* | They are the same, but she still didn't make the shape. |
| *Mr. B.:* | Draw the two blocks on your piece of paper again, and cut them out. [Pause] Only this time lay the paper block D on top of the paper block C, and cut off the part of block C that is sticking out, and see if you can make block D. [The children finished following the directions.] |
| *Taylor:* | They are the same, like when I move this piece over here, it does make a triangle just like this block (block D). But I still don't see how they are the same, because block D is bigger. |
| *Melissa:* | No, they're not they are the same; it doesn't matter how you cut the paper, you get the same shape both times. |
| *Nicole:* | I agree with Melissa, they are the same, so they both are two glue sticks. |
| *Nicholas:* | I agree, they are both two glue sticks, but I don't get it, because this one is bigger like Taylor says, so it gots to be more. |
| *Mr. B.:* | I would like all of you to think about Melissa's solution to the problem some more, but before we quit today, I would like you to solve one more problem. You know that two glue sticks balance block C. How many glue sticks do you predict will balance block J (fig. 3.1)? |

## Experiencing success

I chose to direct the discussion away from block D and toward block J for several reasons. First, we were approaching the end of the school day. Second, block J presented a less challenging problem than block D, and I wanted the children to successfully solve a problem so that their last impression of the activity and of themselves as problem solvers would be positive. Third, I knew that Taylor and Nicholas were not going to readily abandon their misconception that block D was bigger than block C. Like most children, they frequently—

- allow their misconceptions to interfere with new learning,

- are emotionally as well as intellectually attached to their misconceptions,

- will not abandon their misconceptions even in the face of clear evidence that refutes them, and

- will be able to correct their misconceptions only through additional experiences and time for reflection

(Campanario 2002; Watson 1997; Woodward and Howard 1994; Resnick 1983).

Therefore, we resumed our discussion by examining the children's predictions for block J.

> *Nicole:* What I did is, I stacked them up like before, but it was too hard, so I put these ones (four block Cs) beside this one (block J), and they are the same [arranging the blocks as in figure 3.25]. So I think it is "one, two, three, four." No, I did it again, I mean "two, four, six, eight" glue sticks (be)cause it is counting by twos and I don't need to count by ones.
>
> *Nicholas:* I agree (be)cause I did it the same way, only I put them, like, on the flat, not standing up like she did, and I counted with my pen, and it was eight glue sticks [arranging the blocks as shown in figure 3.26].
>
> *Taylor:* I agree, it is eight glue sticks because this one (block G) is four glue sticks because we already know that, and this one (block G) is four glue sticks because we already know that, so 4 + 4 = 8 glue sticks [arranging the blocks as shown in figure 3.27 as he speaks]. So I agree.
>
> *Melissa:* I agree with everybody, we all got it. It's eight glue sticks because I counted like this, "two, four six, eight." As Melissa counted, she took one block C and moved it along the length of block J. Each time she moved block C, she used her pen to draw a line on block J to show where she had last placed block C [marking block J as shown in figure 3.28 as she spoke].

53

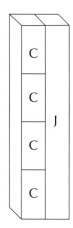

Fig. 3.25. Nicole's upright block arrangement for the problem involving block J

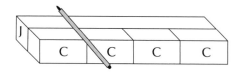

Fig. 3.26. Nicholas's arrangement demonstrating his agreement with Nicole's answer

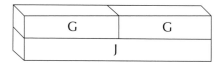

Fig. 3.27. Taylor's alternative arrangement to demonstrate agreement with Nicholas's and Nicole's answer

Fig. 3.28. Melissa's arrangement and markings to demonstrate her agreement with everyone's answer

> *Mr. B.:*   All of you were excellent problem solvers today. Keep thinking about how Melissa solved the problem for block D, and see if her way will work for some of the other blocks on your recording sheet.

## Moving On

The reader may be curious as to why I did not ensure that all the children correctly answered each of the problems throughout the activity before introducing a new problem. One of the challenges teachers face when doing problem solving with young children is to know when to explore a problem more deeply to help children arrive at a correct solution and when to move on to a new problem to give children the chance to experience the mathematical concepts embedded within the problems from a different perspective. My goal when doing these kinds of activities is not to ensure that every child solves every problem correctly but rather to gradually deepen the children's understanding of various mathematical concepts as the activity progresses and ideas are shared and discussed.

The reader may also be curious as to why I did not ask the children to predict the weight of all the blocks shown on the recording sheet (I had skipped blocks F, H, and M). I intentionally omitted some blocks from the discussion so the children could explore parts of the activity on their own and thereby have an opportunity to take responsibility for their own learning.

# Discussion Group 2

## Group 2's Problem

82 plastic cubes balance block A (fig. 3.29). How many plastic cubes do you predict will balance each of the other blocks?

Note: Although only one set of Unit Blocks is shown in figure 3.29, the actual table contained several sets of unit blocks to give each child ready access to all the blocks.

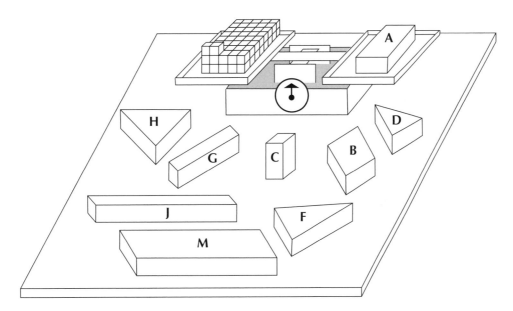

Fig. 3.29. Students are asked to predict the number of plastic cubes that would be required to balance each of the other blocks on the table.

Once again, I asked the four children to form pairs sitting on opposite sides of the table. The table contained several sets of the Unit Blocks, and in the center of the table was a balance with block A balanced by eighty-two plastic cubes. The children in this discussion group documented their predictions using the recording sheet shown in figure 3.30.

One pair of children included Antonio, an ESL third grader having average mathematical abilities, and his partner Lindsey, a second grader performing on grade level in mathematics. The other pair consisted of Ariel, a third grader having above-average mathematical abilities, and her partner Zachery, a second grader performing below grade level in mathematics.

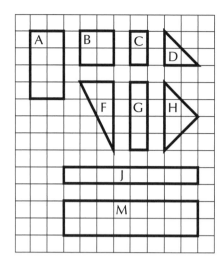

Fig. 3.30. Recording sheet used by the children in discussion group 2

## The Warm-Up

In contrast with the previous discussion group, I chose to place block A on the balance rather than block C. I did so because I wanted these children to think about the blocks in terms of fractional quantities rather than doubling quantities as used with the first discussion group. I began the activity with a warm-up lesson on doubling and halving numbers using mental mathematics.

| | |
|---|---|
| *Mr. B.:* | Before we begin the activity for today, I would like you do some mental math. The first question I would like you to answer is "What is twice as much as 6?" |
| *Lindsey:* | Twelve. |
| *Mr. B.:* | How do you know it is 12? |
| *Lindsey:* | Because what I did is, 5 + 5 is 10, but 6 is 1 more, so you do that twice, so that's 2, and 10 + 2 = 12. So it's 12. |
| *Antonio:* | "I agree because I just know it's 12 because 6 and 6 is 12. |
| *Mr. B.:* | What is twice as much as 16? |
| *Ariel:* | Well, 10 + 10 is 20 and double 6 is 12, so I think it is 32. |
| *Mr. B.:* | How did you know that 20 + 12 is 32? |
| *Ariel:* | Well, 20 + 10 is 30, and 2 more is 32. |
| *Mr. B.:* | What is twice as much as 26? |
| *Zachery:* | What I did is, a quarter is 25 cents and another quarter is 25 cents, |

> and a quarter and a quarter is 50, so it's 2 more (be)cause you got 26 not 25.
>
> *Mr. B.:* I agree with how you solved the problem, but what is your final answer?
>
> *Zachery:* Like I said, it's 52 (be)cause you got to plus 2 more to 50.
>
> *Lindsey:* I agree, only I did it this way. I said "10, 20" (Lindsey held up two fingers on one hand), and then I did it again, "10, 20" (Lindsey held up two more fingers), so that's 10, 20, 30, 40. But, I still need to do the sixes, so 41, 42, 43, 44, 45, 46 [as she counted she held up one finger until she had raised six fingers], that's one; 47, 48, 49, 50, 51, 52 [she again used her fingers as before], that's the other one. So it's 52. I agree.
>
> *Mr. B.:* What is twice 56?
>
> *Antonio:* That's easy (be)cause 50 and 50 is 100, and we already know the 6 and 6 is 12, so it's got to be 112.
>
> *Ariel:* I agree because 50 and 50 is 100, and 6 and 6 is 12, so it is 112.
>
> *Mr. B.:* What is twice 76?
>
> *Ariel:* Well, 50 and 50 is 100, and 20 and 20 is 40, and 6 and 6 is 12, so it's 142. No, wait, I mean 152 (be)cause I forgot to add the 10.
>
> *Zachery:* I agree because 75 cents and 75 cents is a dollar fifty and 2 more is a dollar fifty two. So I agree, it's 152.
>
> *Mr. B.:* "What is one-half of 4?"
>
> *Lindsey:* That's easy, it's 8 because you just hold up four fingers and do it again.

Lindsey's response was very typical of those of young children. Once they get into a pattern of answering certain questions in a particular way, they sometimes have difficulty switching gears and thinking differently about a new question. In this instance, Lindsey listened to only one part of the question because she had already anticipated what the question would ask her to do. I have noticed similar behavior when children answer computation questions on multiple-choice tests. For example, if the test asks children to answer several questions using addition, they might solve the next question using addition even if the question clearly asks them to subtract.

> *Zachery:* I disagree because it's 2, not 8. Half of 4 is 2. You twiced it.
>
> *Lindsey:* I disagree with myself. It is 2 like Zachery said.

| | |
|---|---|
| *Mr. B.:* | What is one-half of 14? |
| *Lindsey:* | I think it might be 7, but I'm not sure, because 6 + 6 is 12, so maybe it's 7 because, let me check, 7 + 7 might be 14 [she counted on from 7 and stopped when she had raised 7 fingers]; it's 7 because 7 + 7 is 14. |
| *Mr. B.:* | What is one-half of 24? |
| *Zachery:* | I know 10 and 10 is 20, so half is 10 and half of 4 is 2, so it's 12. |
| *Antonio:* | I agree because 2 feet is 24 inches and half is 1 foot, so it's 12 inches. |
| *Mr. B.:* | What is one-half of 5? |

This question caused the children to think more deeply than before, and three of the children attempted to solve the problem using paper and pens.

| | |
|---|---|
| *Zachery:* | You can't do it. |
| *Mr. B.:* | What do you mean, "You can't do it"? |
| *Zachery:* | You can't take it in half because there's one too many. See, you know, it's two, but you have one too many. |
| *Ariel:* | I disagree because you can do it. Look, you just divide the extra one in half [making the sketch shown in figure 3.31], so it's 2 and 1/2. |

Fig. 3.31. Ariel's sketch to illustrate her answer of 2 1/2

| | |
|---|---|
| *Zachery:* | I still don't see how it is 2 1/2. |
| *Ariel:* | Zachery you know half of 4 is 2, right? [Zachery nodded his head in agreement.] And you know half of 1 is just a half, right? [Zachery again nodded his head in agreement.] So just put them together because 5 is 4 and 1 if you put them together. |

*Zachery:* But why didn't you pass them out or something?

*Ariel:* Because I could just see it was going to be two on each side and divide the one in the middle in half.

*Mr. B.:* What is half of 15?

*Lindsey:* Well, half of 10 is 5 (be)cause half of ten fingers is five fingers, and Ariel just said half of 5 is 2 1/2, so it's 2 1/2. No, wait, that can't be right (long pause). I'm confused.

At this point Lindsey experienced what brain researchers call *downshifting,* or what I call "deer in the headlights syndrome." She knew her answer was incorrect, but she was unable to see beyond her error and correct it. So I decided to ask her some leading questions.

*Mr. B.:* Lindsey, 15 is the same as what two numbers added together?

*Lindsey:* Ten and 5.

*Mr. B.:* What is one half of 10?

*Lindsey:* Five.

*Mr. B.:* What is one half of 5?

*Lindsey:* Oh, I get it, I didn't add them together. So it's 5, 6, 7 and 1/2.

*Mr. B.:* I agree, one-half of 15 is 7 1/2, so what is one-half of 25?

*Ariel:* It is 12 and 1/2 because 10 + 10 = 20 and 2 1/2 + 2 1/2 is 5, so together that's 25.

*Antonio:* I agree, half of 20 is 10, but what I did is, I drew the 5 like this, and you can't do it because when you pass them out, there is one more than you need [producing a sketch as seen in figure 3.32]. So I cut it in half, so they each got a half, and so I think it is 10 + 2 + 1/2, so that's 12 1/2.

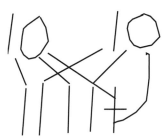

Fig. 3.32. Antonio's drawing to support his answer of 12 1/2

## The Problem-Solving Portion of the Activity

With the warm-up exercise finished, I began the discussion of the problem-solving portion of the activity.

> *Mr. B.:* Yesterday I noticed that Ariel and Zachery discovered that eighty-two plastic cubes balance block A. I have repeated their experiment with the balance on the table, and you can see that Ariel and Zachery were correct. Today I am going to ask you to think like a mathematician. You are going to use Ariel and Zachery's discovery along with what mathematicians call *reasoning* to solve some problems and make some predictions. After you have made each prediction, share with your partner how you found the answer. When you are finished, your partner needs to tell you why she or he agrees or disagrees with what you have done. When everyone is finished sharing with her or his partner, you can explain to the whole group how you solved the problem, and we will comment on your solution or ask you questions. Are there any questions?

*Making a prediction*

> *Lindsey:* What's a prediction?
>
> *Mr. B.:* That's a good question; share with your partner what you think a prediction might be. [The children discussed their definition of a prediction with their partners.]
>
> *Mr. B.:* Lindsey, what do you think a predication is now?
>
> *Lindsey:* Well, I agree with Antonio, it is like what you think the answer is going to be, but you don't know for sure.
>
> *Ariel:* Like, you predict it might rain, but you don't know it will because it might not, but it might.
>
> *Mr. B.:* Why would you think it might rain?
>
> *Ariel:* Because it is cloudy.
>
> *Mr. B.:* So when you make a prediction, you have a reason for thinking something might happen or be true.

Lidsey and the others nodded that they understood the agreed-on meaning of the word *prediction.*

*Mr. B.:*   Here is your first problem. If eighty-two cubes balance block A, how many cubes do you predict will balance block B (fig. 3.29)?

As with the previous group, I held up block B as I posed the problem so that the children could easily locate that block on the table. Three children began to compare the size of block B with that of some of the other blocks on the table, since they seemed to have made the connection that the size of the block was related to its weight. Zachery seemed confused and watched the other children.

## Sharing solutions

*Mr. B.:*   Antonio, would you share first?

*Antonio:*  What's half of 82 is 41 (be)cause 40 and 40 is 80 and 1 and 1 is 2. So I think it is forty-one cubes to make it balance.

*Mr. B.:*   Why did you take one-half of eighty-two cubes?

*Antonio:*  Because this block (block B) is half of this block (block A) when you put them together like this [arranging the blocks as in figure 3.33]. So this one's (block A) eighty-two cubes and this one's (block B) got to be forty-one cubes (be)cause it's half, and half of 82 is 41.

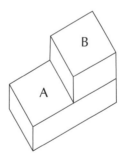

Fig. 3.33. Antonio's block arrangement supporting
his answer of forty-one cubes

*Lindsey:*  I agree (be)cause block B is half as much as block A.

*Mr. B.:*   Lindsey, what do you mean, "block B is half as much as block A"?

*Lindsey:*  Half as much the size, like half as big (be)cause you can just look at it and see it's half as much, so I predict it weighs half as much.

*Antonio:*  Look, if I put one of these (block A) in one hand and one of these (block B) in my other hand, I can tell it weighs half as much. [Like

Melissa in the previous group, Antonio moved his hands up and down as if they were a balance comparing the weights of the two blocks.]

*Mr. B.:*   Antonio, I can see that you can use your hands to tell that block A is heavier than block B because you can feel it weighs more. But how do you know block B weighs one-half as much as block A?

*Antonio:*   Well, because it is half as big (be)cause they are the same tall, but this one (block B) is half as big as this one (block A).

*Mr. B.:*   What do you mean, "they are the same tall"?

*Antonio:*   Look, when you put them beside each other, this one (block A) is as tall as this one (block B) [arranges the blocks as shown in figure 3.34].

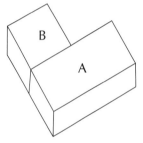

Fig. 3.34. Antonio's arrangement to demonstrate that block A is as "tall" as block B

*Mr. B.:*   So when you say "tall," what do you mean?

*Antonio:*   They are the same thick.

*Mr. B.:*   How are all of the blocks on the table the same?

*Zachery:*   They are all made out of wood.

*Lindsey:*   They are all a shape.

*Mr. B.:*   What do you mean, "They are all a shape"?

*Lindsey:*   They are all squares or triangles or something.

*Mr. B.:*   Do you notice any other shapes?

*Ariel:*   There are rectangles, and that's all.

*Mr. B.:*   Are all of the blocks alike in some other way? [A long pause ensued because the children thought they had found all the ways the blocks were the same.]

> *Antonio:* I'm not sure, but I think they are all the same tall. Like, if you put them beside each other, the tops match up. So I think they are all the same tall.
>
> *Mr. B.:* Antonio has made an important observation about all of the blocks—they do look like they are the same height, or thickness. Everyone, check the blocks to see if you agree or disagree with Antonio's discovery.

The children checked the blocks, and they all agreed that Antonio was correct, although they engaged in some discussion about blocks C, G, and J because the width and height of those blocks was the same.

> *Mr. B.:* Ariel, would you share next?
>
> *Ariel:* I agree with Antonio because if you take two of these blocks (two block Bs) and put them on this block (block A), they match up, so this one (block B) is half of this one (block A). So it (block B) should weigh half as much. So that's half of 82. So it's forty-one cubes.
>
> *Mr. B.:* How do you know one-half of eighty-two cubes is forty-one cubes?
>
> *Ariel:* Well, I split the 82 into two parts, like 80 and 2, and half of 80 is 40 and half of 2 is 1. So then I just put them back together, and it is 41.
>
> *Mr. B.:* Zachery how did you solve this problem?
>
> *Zachery:* I agree because I did it the same way and got 41.

I suspected that Zachery had not solved the problem and instead had chosen to agree with the other children because he believed they had gotten the correct answer. I could have questioned Zachery further at this time, but I chose not to. Rather, I waited to see what he could glean from our discussion about the blocks.

> *Mr. B.:* Next, I would like you to predict how many cubes will balance block C (fig. 3.29).

As the children began to work on this problem, Zachery started to compare the size of block C with that of some of the other blocks on the table, but he remained tentative and seemed confused about what the problem asked him to do. So I asked Lindsey to share first.

> *Lindsey:* If you put these two blocks (two block Cs) together, it will be half of this block (block A) [arranging the blocks as seen in figure 3.35]. So

one of these (block C) is a fourth of this block (block A) (be)cause it would take four of them to make the whole thing. So I think it would be 20 1/2 cubes.

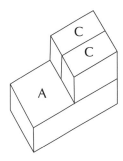

Fig. 3.35. Lindsey's arrangement in support of her answer of 20 1/2 cubes

*Mr. B.:*   How did you know 20 1/2 cubes will balance block C?

*Lindsey:*   Well, what I did was, I went, a fourth of 82 is 20 1/2.

*Mr. B.:*   But how did you know one-fourth of 82 cubes is 20 1/2 cubes?

*Lindsey:*   Because that's the answer.

*Mr. B.:*   But how do you know it is the answer?

*Lindsey:*   Because a fourth of 82 is 20 1/2.

As the reader can observe, Lindsey was using *circular logic,* as discussed previously in this chapter. From past experiences with children, I realized that Lindsey and I could go around and around for a long time. So I asked the other children how they had solved the problem.

*Antonio:*   Well, the other day Brandi and I figured out that a fourth is a half of a half. So you go, half of 82 is 41 (be)cause we already know that (be)cause we just did it with the other block (block B), and so you go, half again, and half of 41 is 20 1/2 because 20 + 20 is 40 and 1/2 + 1/2 is 1.

*Mr. B.:*   Zachery, do you agree or disagree with Antonio?

*Zachery:*   I don't know (be)cause I don't get it. [Zachery's comment showed that he had made a big step in trying to understand the problem—he admitted that he didn't "get it" instead of simply agreeing with the other children as he had previously done.]

*Mr. B.:*   What don't you get?

*Zachery:* I don't know how the blocks help you predict stuff?

*Mr. B.:* Let's see how Ariel solved the problem.

*Ariel:* OK, well I figured that if this (block A) is the block we started balancing, and first we know that this block (block B) is half of this block (block A), and we can put this block (B) on top of this block (A) and see that is half. But now if we put this block (block C) on top of this block (B), it looks like it is half again, and I can prove it by putting another one (block C) on and they are the same as this one (block B) [arranging the blocks as in figure 3.36 as she speaks]. So this block (block C) is like Lindsey said, a half of a half, so it's a fourth, just like she said, and then you would take half of 82 is 41, but to do a fourth you take it in half again, so half of 40 is 20 and half of 1 is 1/2. So it's 20 1/2 cubes. That's how I would do it.

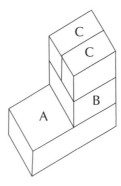

Fig. 3.36. Ariel's block arrangement in support of her answer of 20 1/2 cubes

When Ariel was finished, I checked Zachery's understanding by asking him to explain how Ariel had solved the problem.

*Zachery:* I still don't get it.

*Ariel:* [Looking at Zachery] I can try again. Do you want me to go slower?

*Zachery:* OK.

Ariel repeated her solution, and this time Zachery watched and listened intently to her explanation. At various times, Ariel paused and asked Zachery to explain what she had done up to that point. When she was finished, I once again asked Zachery to summarize how Ariel had solved the problem. This time, Zachery was able to paraphrase Ariel's solution, but with some difficulty.

> *Mr. B.:* Antonio, do you agree with Zachery?
>
> *Antonio:* It's not exactly what I did, but I agree because there's always different ways to do it, and that way works, too. So I agree, he gots it pretty good.
>
> *Mr. B.:* Next, I would like you to predict how many cubes will balance block D (fig. 3.29).

Unlike the younger children in the previous group, these children had little difficulty solving this problem, because its solution represented a natural extension of the strategies they had successfully used so far in the activity (the unknown block is half the size of another block).

## Arriving at agreement

> *Mr. B.:* Antonio, would you share first this time?
>
> *Antonio:* Well, it is kind of like we did before, it is just a different way to cut this block (block B) in half, only you cut it diagonally, not straight like with these blocks (block C). So what I did is, I said it (block D) is half of this one (block B) because when you put it like this [arranges the blocks as in figure 3.37], you can see it is half, only cut different. So it is 20 1/2 cubes to make it balance, just like before.

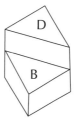

Fig. 3.37. Antonio's block arrangement in support of his answer of 20 1/2 cubes

> *Ariel:* I agree, but I did it this way. We know it takes two block Bs to make the one (block A) we are balancing, because we already did that, and it takes two block Ds to make one block B. So it takes four block Ds to make the one (block A) we are balancing, and I can prove it like this [she positions one block D on top of block A, as in figure 3.38a, then flips block D three times, as in figures 3.38b–d, to show that block D is one-fourth of block A]. So it is 1/4 of 82, and we already know that it (block D) is 20 1/2 cubes because like Antonio said, it is just cut different.

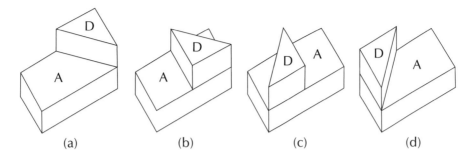

Fig. 3.38. Ariel's arrangement showing flips of a single block D
to show that it is one-fourth of block A

> *Lindsey:* I agree because I did it just like Antonio, and I agree with Ariel that
> it is 20 1/2 cubes.
>
> *Mr. B.* Next I would like you to predict how many cubes will balance block F
> (fig. 3.29).

Block F was the first block that presented a significant challenge for these children. Like the younger children in the previous group who struggled to solve the problem involving block D, these children also attempted to solve this problem using several unsuccessful methods, including the *fill-in* method, as illustrated in figure 3.39, and the *enclosure* method, depicted in figure 3.40.

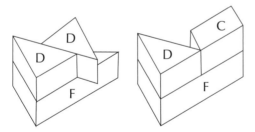 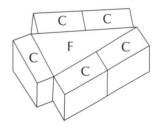

Fig. 3.39. A block arrangement representing children's attempt to solve the block F problem using the fill-in method

Fig. 3.40. A block arrangement representing children's attempt to solve the block F problem using the enclosure method

Other children, including Zachery, did something quite unusual, which will be described after the description of Ariel's and Antonio's solutions.

> *Antonio:* This is hard.
>
> *Mr. B.:* Why is it challenging?
>
> *Antonio:* Because they [referring to the other blocks] don't match up.

> *Mr. B.:* Why don't they match up?
>
> *Antonio:* Because they aren't the right shape. They don't have the right kind of corners.
>
> *Mr. B.:* What do you mean, "They don't have the right kind of corners"?
>
> *Antonio:* They aren't the right kind of [pause], I'm not sure what you call them [long pause], I think it is *angle* or something.

I decided to use Antonio's comment as a jumping off point for a minilesson about some geometric terms. During the minilesson I asked the children to identify examples of right angles, acute angles, and parallelograms using the blocks on the table. When we were done with the minilesson, we resumed our discussion of block F.

> *Mr. B.:* Ariel would you share how you solved this problem?
>
> *Ariel:* OK. What I did was, I said one of these (block F) and another one (block F) makes one of these (block A). So I put them (two block Fs) on top [arranges the blocks as in figure 3.41], and you can see that they match up. And if this one (block A) is eighty-two cubes to balance it, then this one (block F) is half of 82, or 41, because we have already figured out half of 82 is forty-one cubes.

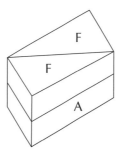

Fig. 3.41. Ariel's block arrangement in support
of her answer of forty-one cubes

> *Lindsey:* I agree (be)cause half of 82 is 41, and it (block F) does cut the other one (block A) in half diagony, just like she said.
>
> *Ariel:* What do you mean, "diagony"?
>
> *Lindsey:* Like, from the corner to a corner.
>
> *Ariel:* Oh, you mean *diagonally*.
>
> *Lindsey:* That's what I said, diagony, I mean, diagonally.

### Dealing with an unexpected approach

> *Antonio:* I agree, but I didn't think to do it that way (be)cause I noticed on the paper that you could use the squares on the paper [referring to the grid on the recording form in figure 3.30 that the children had been given at the start of the activity]. See, two squares is the same as this block (C) that is 20 1/2 cubes to balance it. So that's what two squares is, and this part of the square and this part of the square is about one and the same, for these two parts of a square are about one [illustrates his comment as seen in figure 3.42]. So I thought this would count as one and this would count as one, so I went, "one, two, three, four" squares. So that would make it twice as much as this block (block C). So I thought it would be forty-one cubes.

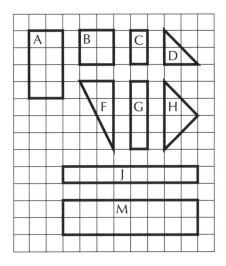
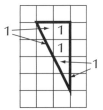

Fig. 3.42

> *Mr. B.:* That is very interesting because Antonio used what mathematicians call a *grid* rather than the blocks to find the answer to the problem. Antonio, would you share again how you solved the problem, because I'm not sure I understood everything you did.

Antonio repeated his explanation, and we all agreed that the grid approach was a very different way of solving the problem. For most children just seeing the correct relationship between the size of the blocks and their weight was a challenge, but for Antonio to have used the grid on the recording sheet to develop those relationships showed real flexibility in his thinking. Interestingly, in this multiage class of thirty-one children, two other children (one third grader and one second grader) used the grid as a solution strategy to solve one or more problems.

## *Challenging a student's incorrect strategy*

> *Mr. B.:*  Zachery, how did you solve the problem?
>
> *Zachery:*  I think you can do it this way. OK, what I did is, I stood this (block F) on here (block A), and it (block F) cuts it (bock A) in half [arranges the blocks as shown in figure 3.43 to demonstrate his solution). So I think this (block A) is 82; then half of 82 is 41 (be)cause half of 100 is 50, but 82 is 18 less (than 100), so it's half of that (18) is 9, so it's 9 less (than 50), so it's 41. So I think it would be forty-one cubes.

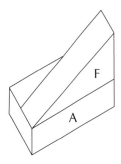

Fig. 3.43. Zachery's arrangement to support his solution of forty-one cubes

In this multiage class, two other children, both first graders, used a similar incorrect strategy to determine the number of objects needed to balance one or more blocks.

None of the children recognized Zachery's error in logic, probably because they fell victim to a behavior common to many young problem solvers—they focused on the answer rather than the solution process, and since Zachery had found the right answer, they assumed that his solution method was also correct. In addition, Zachery's solution did in a way make sense—when block F was stood upright on block A, it did cut block A in half. But this relationship was true only because the height (thickness) of block F just happens to equal one-half the width of block A (as was true of the thickness of all the Unit Blocks on the table). This coincidence allowed Zachery to arrive at the correct answer but for the wrong reason. I chose not to point out Zachery's error in logic at this time, since I wanted to determine whether the children could discover it on their own. Therefore, I asked Zachery to repeat his solution process. But once again, all the children agreed with his solution method. I decided to have Lindsey share her solution, and I hoped the children would notice the significant difference between Zachery's and Lindsey's similar approaches to solving the problem.

*Mr. B.:*  Lindsey, how did you solve this problem?

*Lindsey:*  What I did is, I laid this one (block F) on its side and I put it (block F) here on top of this block (block A), and it (block F) will be half of this block (block A) because it cuts it diagony [arranges the blocks as seen in figure 3.44]. So half of 82 is forty-one cubes, just like Antonio said.

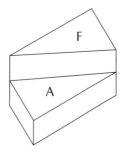

Fig. 3.44. Lindsey's arrangement to support her solution of forty-one cubes

*Ariel:*  I agree (be)cause a half is a half no matter how you cut this one (block A). Because you can cut it different ways and it is still a half, like, you can cut it across like we did with this one (block B), or you can cut it diagonally like this one (block F). But I disagree because you said "diagony" and it is "diagonally."

*Lindsey:*  Oh, yeah, I mean "diagony," no, I mean "diagonally." I have a hard time saying it.

*Mr. B.:*  How are Zachery's and Lindsey's way of solving the problem different?

*Zachery:*  Lindsey has her block flat, and mine is standing up.

*Mr. B.:*  Does it make any difference how you put block F on top of block A?

A long pause followed, and none of the children were able to respond to my question. Perhaps the question seemed silly, because in this instance it really did not matter how one positioned block F on top of block A—one could get the correct answer either way. I chose not to pursue this issue any further, realizing that the error in Zachery's thinking would be difficult to demonstrate using the Unit Blocks that were on the table. Later I realized that perhaps the children could have discovered Zachery's mistake had they been given some blocks with different thicknesses.

## Tackling a more challenging problem

> *Mr. B.:*  The next block I would like you to look at is block H. How many cubes will balance this block (fig. 3.29)?

Block H presented a real challenge for these children, and they struggled to find a successful solution method. Lindsey and Antonio tried to use the *fill-in* method as described previously in this chapter. Zachery repeated the same error in logic by standing block H upright on top of block A. Ariel used two of the H blocks to make a large rectangular prism with a square face, and then she tried to match this prism to one of the other blocks. Children in other groups have attempted to use the *enclosure* method, or they have tried to *fill-in* the rectangular prism that they have made using two of the H blocks.

Up to this point, all the children had chosen to work alone. For this question, though, Antonio and Lindsey started to share materials and work cooperatively after their initial attempts to solve the problem proved unsuccessful. In contrast, Ariel and Zachery continued to work by themselves.

> *Mr. B.:*   Who would like to share first?
>
> *Ariel:*   Well, how I did it is, I used this block (block H) and I also used two of the little triangles (block D), and the first thing I tried is, I tried to see if I could get the two small triangles to make the big triangle (block H), and I managed that [arranges the blocks as seen in figure 3.45]. See, I'll show you, they (two block Ds) go together just like this to make one big triangle (block H). Now I said, well, if you put these two small triangles (two block Ds) together a different way, they make a square like this block (block B) [now arranges the blocks as seen in figure 3.46]. And we figured out that it (block B) was half of this block (block A). So either way, it's going to be 41 because this one (block B) we know is 41, and half of this one (block A) is half of 82, which is forty-one cubes. See, you get it no matter what you do.
>
> *Zachery:*  I don't get it.
>
> *Ariel:*   You know that this one (block B) is forty-one cubes because it is half of 82. [Zachery nods in agreement.] And these two blocks (two block Ds) are the same as this one (block B), so together they make 41, too. [Again Zachery nods in agreement, but he seems less sure of himself.] And if we just turn them (two block Ds) a different way, they make this one (block H). So it (block H) must be forty-one

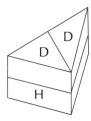

Fig. 3.45. Ariel's block arrangement to show that two block Ds match one block H

Fig. 3.46. Ariel's block arrangement to show that two block Ds also match one block B

cubes, too, because they are all the same. [Zachery now seems even more unsure, but he nods in agreement anyway.]

*Mr. B.:* Lindsey and Antonio, would you share how you solved this problem.

*Antonio:* Well, what we did is, we put two of them (two block Hs) together, and made a square, but it didn't match. So we tried something different, and we put the blocks on top of the A block like this [arranges the blocks as shown in figure 3.47]. And this one (block D) is a fourth, and this one (block D) is a fourth, and this one (block H) must be two-fourths because 1/4 and 1/4 and 2/4 makes a whole.

*Lindsey:* And this (block D) and this (block D) make a half of this (block A), so this (block H) must be a half, too, because a half and a half make one whole. So it's forty-one cubes.

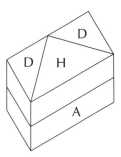

Fig. 3.47. Antonio and Lindsey's arrangement in support of their solution of forty-one cubes

I thought that Antonio's failure to use the grid to solve this problem was interesting, in that the area of block H could more easily be determined by using the grid than by comparing it with the area of block F, because the partial squares on the grid for block H are cut evenly in half (see fig. 3.48). Children sometimes apply a strategy in a situation in which the strategy is difficult to use, yet overlook the strategy in situations in which it could more easily be used to arrive at the solution.

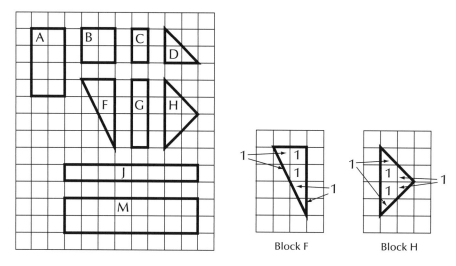

Fig. 3.48. The area of block H could more easily be determined using the grid than by directly comparing it with the area of block F.

*Zachery:* I kind of get it, but I still don't know what blocks to use, (be)cause there are lots of them on the table.

*Mr. B.:* I agree, sometimes the hardest part of solving a problem is getting started, but it always helps to be patient and try different things until you find something that works. It also helps to work with a partner like Antonio and Lindsey just did.

*Lindsey:* Like, at first we tried to use two of the big triangles (two block Hs) to make them fit on this one (block A). But it didn't work, so we kept trying until we got it.

*Antonio:* Then we couldn't get it (be)cause when we put this one (block H) on top of this one (block A), we tried to use ones like this (block C) and they wouldn't work, and so we tried a whole bunch of them until it worked.

*Mr. B.:* The last block we are going to investigate is block J. How many cubes will balance block J (fig. 3.29)?

*Antonio:* This (block G) is half of this (block J), and this (block C) is 1/4 of this (block J), and another one (block C) is 1/4 again. So when you put them together, they make the whole thing (block J) [arranges the blocks as seen in fig. 3.49].

*Lindsey:* But like we did before, you can put them a different way, like this [arranges the blocks as in figure 3.50]. And that's eghty-two cubes. So this (block J) is 82 (be)cause the blocks (block A and block J) are the same. Glue them (blocks G, C, and C) together different ways, and you get them (block A or J).

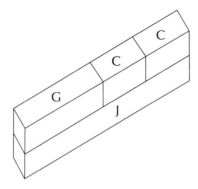
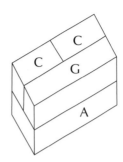

Fig. 3.49. Antonio's arrangement for the problem involving block J

Fig. 3.50. Lindsey's block arrangement in support of her solution of eighty-two cubes for block J

*Zachery:* I agree with eighty-two cubes, but I did it a different way. I noticed two of these (two block Gs) make the same as this (block J), and when you put them on this one (block A), they are the same again. So they are all the same [arranges the blocks as shown in figure 3.51].

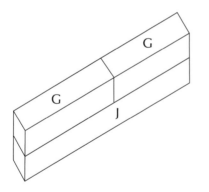
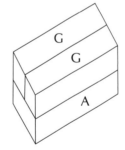

Fig. 3.51. Zachery's alternative block arrangement in support of the solution of eighty-two cubes

*Mr. B.:* What do you mean, "they are all the same"?

*Zachery:* This one (block J) and this one (block A) are the same (be)cause you can make them with the same blocks (two block Gs). So they are both [pause], eighty-two cubes will balance both of them (be)cause they are the same.

*Ariel:* I agree with Zachery because this one (block J) is twice as much as this one (block G), and this one (block A) is twice as much as this one (block G). So that would mean this one (block J) and this one (block A) are the same because they're both twice as much as the same thing. So that's eighty-two cubes.

## Checking an agreed-on solution

Mr. B.: You have all done a great job today. When you go back to your desks, don't forget to make a prediction for the other blocks on the chart. But before you leave, I have one more question. You predicted that it will take 20 1/2 cubes to balance block C. How could you check this prediction, since we do not have any plastic cubes that are cut in half?

Antonio: We could bring a saw to school and cut a cube in half.

Mr. B.: That would work, but can you think of a way to do this without cutting any of the cubes in half?

The children thought about this question for a very long time while I waited. I have learned that sometimes I need to be very patient before children will offer a unique response. In this instance Zachery finally said, "I remember the other day that Eli said that two cards would balance one cube, so if we use one card, it would be the same as half a cube." The other children agreed that Zachery's idea would work, and I asked the children to see whether they could find other things that weighed the same as one half of a cube.

## Concluding thoughts on discussion group 2

Unlike their younger counterparts who composed the first group, the older children in this group showed more flexibility in adopting new strategies when a previously used strategy proved unsuccessful for solving a problem. One of the biggest steps that children can take in becoming better problem solvers is to develop the ability to think flexibly in different situations. Beginning problem solvers are very prone to trying to adapt a previously used strategy to new problems instead of seeking out more appropriate strategies through the use of inventive thinking.

Although all the children demonstrated good skills as problem solvers, Zachery's performance was most commendable throughout the activity. He displayed all the characteristics of a good problem solver—patience, perseverance, and a positive attitude. He did not give up on himself or the activity. In contrast, some children who experience difficulty at the beginning of a lesson simply stop trying, thereby benefiting little from their interactions with the teacher or the other children. Zachery showed real promise as a problem solver—he was not willing to let his initial lack of success serve as a barrier to the positive contributions that he made later in the discussion. He was willing to fail, but he was not willing to be a failure.

# Predicting How Many Pattern Blocks Will Balance a Wooden Unit Block
## Reasoning to Learn, Learning to Reason

Many a guess has turned out to be wrong but never the less useful in leading to a better one.

—George Pólya
*How to Solve It*

Just as music comes alive in the performance of it, the same is true of mathematics. The symbols on the page have no more to do with mathematics than the notes on a page of music. They simply represent the experience.

—Keith Devlin
*Mathematics: The Science of Patterns:*
*The Search for Order in Life*

Pᴿᴼᴮᴸᴱᴹˢ similar to those used in chapter 3 were posed during the activities described in this chapter, but this time the children used pattern blocks rather than glue sticks or plastic cubes as nonstandard units of measurement. Once again the discussions took place among four children and myself as we sat at a table on which were located a balance and four large tubs containing pattern blocks, one tub for each child. While the four children and I worked at the table, the other children in the class were busy authoring pages for a class book of mathematics riddles.

# Anticipating Students' Thinking

The following activities were designed to stretch the children's thinking without making the activity seem overwhelming. I used my firsthand knowledge of the children's mathematical skills and abilities to gauge the level of difficulty for each question and to guide the direction of the discussions. Although I did not have a predetermined plan for the outcome of the discussions, on the basis of my previous experiences with children I had formed a mental outline of directions the discussions might take. In an issue of NCTM *Mathematics Education Dialogues*, Ted Watanabe (2001) referred to such an outline as "anticipating children's thinking." I have found that when I anticipate how children will respond to problems, I can pose better questions that unlock children's existing knowledge and can orchestrate more productive discussions that build on that knowledge.

Interestingly, the children in the following two discussion groups demonstrated a preference for using one of two methods for solving most problems:

- Some children started with the known reference shape—the pattern-block shape on the balance—and then *filled it in* using the pattern block shape for which the problem asked them to solve. They referred to their approach as the "match it up" or "stack it up" method.

- Other children started with the pattern-block shape that the problem asked them to solve for, then "made" the reference pattern-block shape on the balance. They called their approach the "put it together" or "puzzle" method.

Also interesting to note is the fact that some children used the answers to previously solved problems as aids when solving new problems. Doing so facilitated their solution of new problems and helped them find the answers more efficiently.

# Discussion Group 3

The children in discussion group 3 were Andrea, a first grader having average mathematical abilities; Andrea's partner, Timothy, a second grader having low mathematical skills; Jonathan, a first grader having average mathematical abilities; and Jonathan's partner, Mckenzie, a second grader performing on grade level in mathematics. I began the discussion with the following comments.

## Setting the Stage

> *Mr. B.:* The other day I noticed that Andrea and Timothy discovered that 4 hexagons balance this wooden block. I have repeated their experiment using the balance on the table [calling the children's attention to the balance setup as seen in figure 4.1], and you can see

that 4 hexagons do balance this block. I have also written on a card the name of the pattern-block shape that is on the balance.

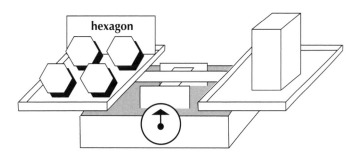

Fig. 4.1. Initial balance arrangement, in which 4 hexagonal pattern blocks balance a given wooden block

*Mr. B.:* Andrea and Timothy's discovery is very important because it lets you think like a mathematician. Mathematicians use what they know to find out new things by making predictions. So today you are going to make some predictions, just like a mathematician. Here is the first question: How much does the wooden block on the balance weigh? [A long pause ensued, after which I continued with another question.] How many hexagons weigh the same as the wooden block?

*Jonathan:* Four.

*Mr. B.:* Four what?

*Jonathan:* Four of those [points to the hexagonal pattern blocks on the balance].

*Mr. B.:* How do you know that?

*Andrea:* Because they balance.

*Mr. B.:* How does that prove they weigh the same?

*Timothy:* Because when they balance, they are equal, because that's how a balance works. You put something on one side and then you put something on the other side, and when it balances, they weigh the same.

*Mckenzie:* Like, the block weighs the same as the hexagons, but we don't know what it is—like, we don't know if it's 1 pound or 2 pounds or what. But we know they are the same.

> *Mr. B.:* Jonathan, do you know the name of the pattern-block shape on the balance?
>
> *Jonathan*: I know it, but I can't think of the name.
>
> *Mr. B.:* Does everyone know the names of all of the pattern-block shapes?
>
> *Andrea:* I don't know the red one and the blue one and the yellow one.
>
> *Jonathan:* I know all the names, but I don't know which one they go to.

## Warming Up

At this point I began the warm-up part of the activity, which was to review the names of the pattern-block shapes. After our discussion, I made this request: "When we are done, I would like Andrea and Jonathan to get their learning logs and write down the names of all of the pattern blocks along with a drawing of each one. I will meet with you next week and see if you have learned the names of each shape. Timothy and Mckenzie will help you spell the names and make the drawings."

Perhaps at this point the reader may be asking why I am having the children solve problems using manipulatives (i.e., pattern blocks) for which some of the children in the group did not know the names of the shapes—should all the children not first be fluent in the use of the shape names *before* they are asked to solve problems using those shapes? Although such is the conventional wisdom, I have found that just the opposite is true—children can learn the names of the shapes through problem-solving activities because the discussion will provide them with a meaningful context to learn and practice the name of each shape.

I believe that the lack of certain types of knowledge should not serve as a limiting factor in children's attempts to engage in sense making when challenged to think critically and creatively about problematic situations. The following discussions show that even though some of the children did not know the names of the pattern-block shapes, they were quite adept at solving problems that required them to use their informal mathematical knowledge to think about the algebraic and geometric relationships that were represented by the shapes.

## Fostering Internal versus External Knowledge

When planning instruction, teachers need to recognize the difference between what Piaget called *external* and *internal knowledge*. Recent researchers have referred to those two types of knowledge as *declarative* and *procedural* (Butterfield 2001). Knowledge that is based solely on social conventions or customs is considered to be external, or declarative, knowledge. It is acquired from sources outside the learner, such as the teacher, other students, books, television, the Internet, and so on. Declarative knowledge is usually transmitted to children by simply telling them what they need to remember, then reinforcing that information through drill and practice. Such knowledge is useful only when it has been committed to memory, and if one forgets it, one cannot figure it out using reason, logic, and proof. For example, the names and spellings of the pattern-block shapes are based on social conventions and customs. No logical reason exists for pronouncing or spelling some of those words the way we do. As an example, the pronunciation of two pattern-block shapes seems quite arbitrary—*hexagon* is pronounced with an irregular sound for the letter *a* (\ä\) that is neither the short \a\ nor long \ā\ sound used in most words. Similarly, the word rhombus contains the silent letter h, which is not pronounced at all and which appears to serve no purpose other than to make the spelling of the word more difficult.

In contrast, internal, or procedural, knowledge is acquired by children as they use their own intuitive capabilities to make sense of information and find solutions for problems. Anyone who has worked with young children realizes how difficult it is to transfer understanding to young learners. Children appear to construct understanding when engaged in problem-solving activities using their own internal resources, such as the ability to analyze, synthesize, and apply information. Problem solving is inherently a sense-making activity that requires children to—

- construct understanding as they struggle to comprehend the mathematical concepts embedded within problems,

- wrestle with the challenges of communicating their solutions clearly and completely to others, and

- reflect on the feedback they receive from others.

Teachers can demonstrate strategies and algorithms for solving problems, but such procedures often appear to children as arbitrary sets of rules that make little or no sense. Teachers can explain *how* procedures work, but children have to make sense of *why* they work and *when* they are most useful. As James Hiebert has pointed out,

> As students develop their own methods for solving problems, they develop general approaches for inventing specific procedures or adapting ones they already know to fit new problems. In other words, they learn how to construct their own methods.
>
> (Hiebert et al. 1997, p. 24)

The principle that should guide mathematics teaching is that children need to understand what they are doing as they simultaneously learn the social conventions of mathematics. "Learning mathematics is a cumulative process, and if you fail to understand one stage, then anything that is built on that stage is going to be rather fragile" (Butterfield 2001, p. 18).

## Engaging in Collaborative Problem Solving

Our discussion continued as I posed the following question:

> *Mr. B.:*    If you know that 4 hexagons balance this block, what else do you know about the other pattern blocks on the table? For example,

what do you know about a trapezoid? [As I spoke, I showed the children a trapezoidal pattern block. Then I placed a trapezoidal block in front of each child and repeated the question. A long pause ensued as the children thought about the question.]

## Sharing solution strategies

*Andrea:* It's the same as 3 triangles.

*Mr. B.:* What do you mean, a trapezoid is "the same as 3 triangles"?

*Andrea:* It's the same shape when you put them (the 3 triangles) together.

*Timothy:* They aren't exactly the same thing, (be)cause the triangles are cut up, but you can put them together and they are the same shape.

*Mr. B.:* What do you know about a trapezoid?

*Timothy:* It's half of one of these [points to the hexagonal pattern blocks on the balance].

*Mr. B.:* What do you mean, "one of these"?

*Timothy:* A hexagon.

*Mr. B.:* Timothy, how do you know a trapezoid is one-half of a hexagon?

*Timothy:* Because if you lay one of these (trapezoidal pattern block) on top of one of these (hexagonal pattern block) [placing a trapezoidal pattern block on top of a hexagonal pattern block], you can see it is half.

*Mr. B.:* Today when you share your answers with your partner or the whole group, I would like you to use the names of the pattern-block shapes.

*Jonathan:* What if you don't know the names?

*Mr. B.:* Say what you think the name is, and then we will help you.

*Mr. B.:* What else do you know about a trapezoid?

*Mckenzie:* If you were balancing this block, you could use 8 of these [holding up a trapezoidal pattern block] to balance that [pointing to the wooden block on the balance].

*Mr. B.:* Remember, we are going to try to use the names of the shapes.

*Mckenzie:* I mean 8 trapezoids would balance the block on the balance.

*Mr. B.:*  How do you know 8 trapezoids would balance the block on the balance?

*Mckenzie:*  Because that [pointing to a hexagonal pattern block on the balance] is 2 of these [pointing to a trapezoidal pattern block], so it's 1, 2 [pause], 3, 4 [pause], 5, 6 [pause], 7, 8 [pointing to the hexagonal pattern blocks on the balance as she counted].

*Mr. B.:*  Mckenzie I would like you to repeat your solution, and this time use the names of the shapes so we can better understand how you solved the problem. [Mckenzie repeated her solution process, and this time she used the terms *hexagon* and *trapezoid* in her explanation.]

*Andrea:*  I agree with Mckenzie. I think it would be 8. I knew both of these [pause]—what are they called? [Mckenzie prompts, "trapezoids"]— would be a hexagon [looking at the card on the balance], and then I added them to see how many halves that would make, and it's 8 if you put them together to make that same shape that I showed you—8 of them (trapezoids) makes 4 of them (hexagons).

*Mr. B.:*  Andrea, let me make sure I understand. You think it is 8 trapezoids because when you put 2 trapezoids together, they make the same shape as a hexagon. So 1 trapezoid is one-half of a hexagon, and if you add up all to the halves in four hexagons, you get 8 halves, or 8 trapezoids.

*Andrea:*  Yeah, I added up the halves.

*Jonathan:*  I agree (be)cause it's kind of how I did it, only I looked at it (hexagon), and half of it (hexagon) is the red one (trapezoid). So, I went, "Cut, cut, cut, cut," and I counted the pieces, and there was 8 pieces.

*Mr. B.:*  How could Jonathan tell us how he solved the problem using the names of the shapes?

*Mckenzie:*  He cut the hexagons in half and counted the pieces that were really trapezoids, and so it is 8 trapezoids.

*Timothy:*  The way I did it was, I went, "Four 2s" because the hexagon is 2 of those [Mckenzie starts to say something, and Timothy continues], I mean 2 trapezoids, and I went, "Four 2s is 8" (be)cause 2 times 4 is 8 trapezoids.

*Mr. B.:*  How do you know 2 times 4 equals 8?

*Timothy:*  Because it's just like counting by 2s, only you go four times, like, "2, 4, 6, 8." See, I went, "Four 2s."

> **Mr. B.:** If you know that 4 hexagons balance this block, what do you know about the shape called a rhombus? [As before, I showed the children a rhomboidal pattern block, placed a rhomboidal pattern block in front of each child, and repeated the question. Then I waited as the children solved the problem with a drawing or by using pattern blocks.]
>
> **Andrea:** It's the same as 2 triangles.
>
> **Mr. B.:** What is the same?
>
> **Andrea:** The shape when you hook the triangles together.
>
> **Timothy:** You could figure out how many rhombus balance the block.
>
> **Mr. B.:** That's a very interesting problem. Everyone, solve Timothy's problem and predict how many rhombi will balance the block, and then share your solution with your partner.
>
> **Mckenzie:** What's a *rhombi?*
>
> **Mr. B.:** That's a very good question. Rhombi are more than one rhombus. When you have more than one of something, you usually add an "s" or "es" to the end of the word. But with some words, you change how you say the word when there is more than one. For example, one goose is a goose, but if you have more than one goose, what would you say?
>
> **Jonathan:** Geese.
>
> **Mr. B.:** Can you think of any other words that change the way you say the word when you have more than one?
>
> **Mckenzie:** Mice because just one is mouse. Like, I have a mouse in my house.
>
> **Andrea:** Hey, that rhymes.
>
> **Mr. B.:** Well, if you have one rhombus, you just say "rhombus," but if you have more than one rhombus, you say "rhombi."

## Comparing solution strategies

After the children solved the problem and shared their solutions with their partner, we resumed our discussion.

> **Jonathan:** Well, I made this drawing [displays a sketch like that shown in figure 4.2], and I counted it four times—"1, 2, 3 [pause], 4, 5, 6 [pause], 7, 8, 9 [pause], 10, 11, 12." So it's 12.

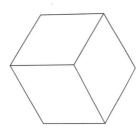

Fig. 4.2. Jonathan's drawing in support of his response that 12 rhombi
(i.e., rhomboidal pattern blocks) would balance the wooden block

| | |
|---|---|
| *Mr. B.:* | Twelve what? |
| *Jonathan:* | Twelve of the [pause] these [Timothy interjects, "rhombus"]. Yeah, 12 rhombuses. |
| *Mr. B.:* | I disagree. Instead of saying "rhombuses," what is the word for more than one rhombus? |
| *Jonathan:* | I forget. |
| *Timothy:* | I think he said "rhombi" or something like that. |
| *Mr. B.:* | I agree, we say "rhombi" when there are more than one rhombus. |
| *Andrea:* | But I disagree because it's 16, not 12. |
| *Mr. B.:* | Andrea, how did you solve the problem? |
| *Andrea:* | I said 2 of those rhombuses make this 1 (trapezoid), and so you count by 2s, not 1's. So I went, "2, 4 [pause], 6, 8 [pause], 10, 12 [pause] 14, 16" [pointing to the 8 trapezoids she had used to solve the previous problem]. |
| *Timothy:* | I disagree because I agree with Jonathan, it should be 12 because 2 rhombus don't make a trapezoid, it's too big—they're not the same. Here, let me show you [arranges blocks as in figure 4.3]. See, it's a triangle, too big [placing the trapezoid on top of the two rhombi so that the blocks were then arranged as shown in figure 4.4]. |

Fig. 4.3. Timothy's block arrangement to show
that "2 rhombus [sic] don't make a trapezoid,
it's too big."

Fig. 4.4. Timothy's block arrangement
in support of his statement "See, it's
a triangle, too big."

> *Mr. B.:*   How many rhombi do make a trapezoid? [This question seemed to be difficult for the children, and they thought about it using the pattern blocks as a tool to help arrive at a solution.]
>
> *Timothy:*   One and part of 1.
>
> *Mckenzie:*   It's 1 1/2 diamonds because this much here is half a diamond, like, half the diamond is there and the other half is cut off.
>
> *Mr. B.:*   Mckenzie, I know some people call this shape a *diamond*, but most mathematicians call it a *rhombus*. So how could you use Andrea's way to get the correct answer?
>
> *Mckenzie:*   I think she should have counted by 1 1/2 or something, not by 2s.
>
> *Mr. B.:*   How much does 1 1/2 plus 1 1/2 equal?
>
> *Timothy:*   Three.
>
> *Mr. B.:*   How did you know that?
>
> *Timothy:*   It's easy—1 and 1 is 2, and 1/2 and 1/2 is 1 more, so it's 3.
>
> *Mr. B.:*   What if you added 1 1/2 eight times. How much would that equal?

The children used their pens and paper or the pattern-block shapes to answer the question. When they were done, we resumed our discussion.

> *Mckenzie:*   It's 12 because it goes, "1 1/2 plus 1 1/2 is 3, plus another 1 1/2 is 4 1/2, plus another 1 1/2 is 6, plus another 1 1/2 is 7 1/2, plus another 1 1/2 is 9, plus another 1 1/2 is 10 1/2, plus another 1 1/2 is 12."
>
> *Timothy:*   There's a easier way because these 2 trapezoids make 3 and so do all the other ones (pairs of trapezoids), so it's "3, 6, 9, 12."
>
> *Mr. B.:*   Two trapezoids make 3 what?
>
> *Timothy:*   Three rhombuses [pause]. What is it called?
>
> *Mckenzie:*   Rhombi.
>
> *Timothy:*   Oh, yeah, 3 rhombuses, I mean 3 rhombi, make a hexagon like this [produces a sketch as seen in figure 4.5]. So you just count the threes, and it's "3, 6, 9, 12" rhombuses. I mean rhombi.
>
> *Mr. B.:*   Now I'm going to take everything off the balance and put a different block on one side of the balance, and I would like you to count as I put some trapezoids on the other side of the balance.

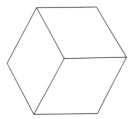

Fig. 4.5. Timothy's sketch to illustrate his response that "3 rhombi make a hexagon."

The children discovered that 9 trapezoids were needed to balance the new block. In the tray containing the trapezoids, I also placed a folded card with the word trapezoid written on both sides, as shown in figure 4.6.

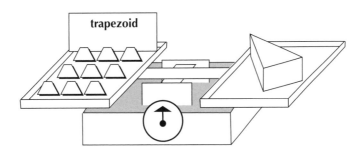

Fig. 4.6. Our second balance arrangement, in which 9 trapezoidal pattern blocks balance a given wooden block

## Tackling a more challenging problem

Mr. B.:    If 9 trapezoids balance this block, how many hexagons will balance this block? [The children solved the problem, shared their solutions with their partner, and told why they agreed or disagreed with each other's solutions.]

Andrea:    I think it would be 4 1/2 because what I did first, I drew 9 lines, and I circled them into groups of 2, and I saw there was 1 left over; so that's 4 1/2 [makes a sketch like that in figure 4.7 as she speaks].

Timothy:   I agree because I got the same answer.

Mr. B.:    Andrea, why did you draw 9 lines?

Andrea:    Because there are 9 of these, I mean trapezoids.

Mr. B.:    Why did you circle 2 lines each time?

Fig. 4.7. Andrea's sketch to illustrate her response that 4 1/2 hexagonal pattern blocks would balance the wooden block

*Andrea:* Because 2 of these (trapezoids) make this 1 (hexagon).

*Mr. B.:* Do you remember the names of the shapes?

*Andrea:* Well, the ones on the balance are trapezoids because the sign says so, and I think this one is a heck something.

*Timothy:* You were so close; it's a hexagon. I did it with a drawing. I drew 9 trapezoids and put them inside the hexagons, but there is 1 left. But the 1 left is half a hexagon, so it's 4 1/2 hexagons.

*Mckenzie:* I agree because Jonathan and I did it the same way, and we got 4 1/2. But, Jonathan thought you wrote 4 1/2 this way [writes the quantity as shown in figure 4.8]. But I showed him the right way to write it.

$$\frac{4}{2}$$

Fig. 4.8. At first, Mckenzie's partner thought the mixed number 4 1/2 was written this way; she then showed him the correct way to write it.

*Mr. B.:* If 9 trapezoids balance this block, how many rhombi will balance this block? [The children were truly challenged by this problem, and they spent a considerable amount of time trying to solve it.]

*Timothy:* You can't do it, because you'd have to use a triangle with this one (rhomboidal pattern block), and you said, "rhombus," not "triangle," but you can't make a half out of a rhombus. I kept trying, but it wouldn't work.

*Jonathan:* I disagree because it did work, like, I think it is 13 1/2 rhombus, but I'm not sure because it is hard.

*Mr. B.:* Why is it challenging?

*Jonathan:* Because like Timothy said, you got one more of these (rhomboidal pattern block), but it doesn't make a [pausing to look at the card on the balance] trapezoid.

*Mr. B.:* Jonathan, so how did you solve the problem?

*Jonathan:* Well, I put the [again looking at the card on the balance] trapezoids together to make the [looking at the card on the table] hexagons, and I put these (rhomboidal pattern blocks) on top like this [arranges the pattern blocks as shown in Figure 4.9]. And I put a one of these (rhomboidal pattern blocks) and a triangle on the last one, and I counted them (rhomboidal pattern blocks) and got 13 1/2.

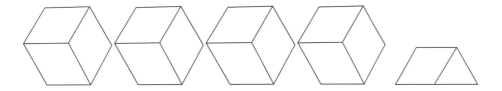

Fig. 4.9. Jonathan's block arrangement to support his answer that 13 1/2 rhombi (rhomboidal pattern blocks) balance the same wooden block as 9 trapezoids (trapezoidal pattern blocks)

## Asking probing questions

*Mr. B.:* How did you know that a triangle was one-half of a rhombus?

*Jonathan:* Because 2 triangles is a rhombus, and if you take 1 triangle away, it's half of it (rhomboidal pattern block).

*Mr. B.:* So let me be sure I understand. If 2 triangles make a rhombus, then 1 triangle is one-half of a rhombus.

*Jonathan:* I agree.

*Mckenzie:* I agree with Jonathan (be)cause I kind of did it the same way. I knew 3 rhombus make a hexagon if you put them together. So it's "1, 2, 3 [pause], 4, 5, 6 [pause], 7, 8, 9 [pause], 10, 11, 12," and that is 8 trapezoids, and then I needed to do a trapezoid, and we knew from the last one (problem) it's 4 1/2 hexagons, so I had to use 1 1/2 rhombus because like Jonathan said, a trapezoid is a rhombus and a half a rhombus. So it's 13 1/2 rhombus.

*Andrea:*    I agree because I got the same answer, but I didn't do it like they did. You got 9 [looking at the card on the balance] trapezoids, and I put a [pause]—what's this? [Timothy prompts, "rhombus"]—I put a rhombus on each one, but it didn't work because there was some left over. So I pushed them (trapezoids) together so they would fit like this [arranges the blocks as shown in figure 4.10].

Fig. 4.10. Andrea's block arrangement in which she had pushed the 9 trapezoidal pattern blocks together

*Andrea:*    Then I put one of these [pause]—what's this? [Mckenzie and Timothy both say, "rhombus"]—rhombus on each [looking at the card on the balance] trapezoid, just like I did the first time [placing one rhomboidal pattern block on top of each trapezoidal pattern block so that the blocks were then arranged as in figure 4.11].

Fig. 4.11. Andrea's pattern block arrangement after she had placed one rhomboidal pattern block on top of each trapezoidal pattern block

*Andrea:*    Then I put on the rest of the rhombus and counted them [filling in the empty spaces with rhombi as seen in figure 4.12]. And I got 13, but there is a half a rhombus, so it's 13 1/2.

Fig. 4.12. Andrea's block arrangement after she had filled in the blank spaces with rhomboidal pattern blocks, demonstrating her agreement with Jonathan's answer: 13 1/2

> *Mr. B.:* That is very interesting. How did you know to put the trapezoids together in a row?
>
> *Andrea:* I don't know. I just did it.
>
> *Mr. B.:* How did you know there was one-half of a rhombus at the end of the row?
>
> *Andrea:* Well, I just looked at, it and it looked like it was half.

## Encouraging Reflection

> *Mr. B.:* You are all great problem solvers. Jonathan and Andrea, be sure to write the names of the pattern-block shapes in your learning logs along with a drawing of each shape so we can talk about them next week.

# Discussion Group 4

The children in this group were Brandi, a second grader having good mathematical abilities; Brandi's partner, Dallas, a third grader performing on grade level in mathematics; Austin, a second grader and a TAG (talented and gifted) student; and Austin's partner, Hillary, a third grader having low mathematical skills.

## Warming Up

Before I began the activity, I used a short warm-up lesson to engage the children in a discussion of some geometric terms. Our discussion was similar to that described with the preceding group, but in addition it included the identification of blocks having right angles, acute angles, and obtuse angles and those whose faces were parallelograms. When the discussion was over, I presented the first problem to the children.

## Engaging in Collaborative Problem Solving

> *Mr. B.:* The other day I noticed that Brandi and Dallas discovered that 28 rhombi balance this wooden block. I have repeated their experiment using the balance on the table, and you can see that 28 rhombi do balance the block. I have also written the word *rhombus* on a card because that is the name of the shape on the balance [calling the children's attention to the balance setup as seen in figure 4.13].

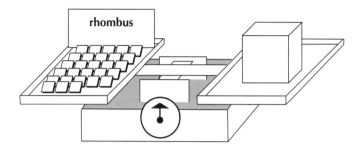

Fig. 4.13. A third balance arrangement, in which 28 rhomboidal pattern blocks balance a given wooden block

## Setting the stage

| | |
|---|---|
| *Mr. B.:* | What Brandi and Dallas have discovery is very important because you can use this information to learn new things. When you know something is true, you can use what you know to make predictions about other things. So today you are going to make some predictions, just like a mathematician. Here is the first question I would like you to think about. How much does the wooden block weigh? |
| *Hillary:* | Well, we don't really know, because a balance isn't like a scale. |
| *Mr. B.:* | How are they different? |
| *Hillary:* | Well, a balance tells you if they are the same, and a scale tells you the weight. |
| *Austin:* | Yeah, like Hillary says, a scale tells you the weight, but a balance only tells you the weight if you already know how much one of the things weighs. Like, if we know the block weighs 2 pounds, then we would know the pattern blocks weigh 2 pounds. |
| *Mr. B.:* | That is very interesting. Let me ask you a couple of questions to see if I understand what you mean. Let's pretend I take the block and the 28 rhombi off the balance. Then, on one side of the balance I put a smaller block that weighs 24 ounces. Next, I discover that 16 rhombi will balance this block. How much does each rhombus weigh? [The children worked on the problem using the pattern blocks and their pens and paper.] |
| *Austin:* | I kind of did a guess and check. I drew the 24 ounces and put them in groups of two, and that didn't work because I needed 16 groups, not 12. So I know it's not groups of one. So I tried groups of three, |

> but that didn't work because I got 8 groups. So then I tried groups of one and a half, and it worked. I checked it, and it's 1 1/2 (ounces) [produces the sketch shown in figure 4.14 as he speaks].

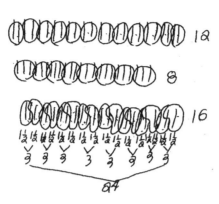

Fig. 4.14. Austin's sketch to show that each rhomboidal pattern block weighs 1 1/2 ounces

| | |
|---|---|
| *Brandi:* | I agree because I did it the same way, and I got 1 1/2 ounces. |
| *Mr. B.:* | Hillary, in Austin's drawing, what are the lines? |
| *Hillary:* | They are the ounces. |
| *Mr. B.:* | Dallas, in Austin's drawing, what are the circles? |
| *Dallas:* | Those are the rhombuses, like, there are 16 of them, just like you said. |
| *Mr. B.:* | I know lots of people use the word *rhombuses* to mean more than one rhombus. But today I would like you to use the word that mathematicians use, which is *rhombi*. |
| *Mr. B.:* | Brandi, how did Austin know 1 1/2 ounces was the weight of each rhombus? |
| *Brandi:* | Because he had 16 of them, and you said that 16 rhombus balance the block, and they are the same; so they both have to be 24 ounces, and they are. |

*Sharing solution strategies*

> *Mr. B.:* Now I'm going to put the block and the rhombi we started with

back on the balance. There are 28 rhombi on the balance. If each rhombus weighs 1 1/2 ounces, how much does the block weigh? [The children worked on the problem.]

*Dallas:* That's easy because 28 × 1 = 28, everyone knows that, and 28 × 1/2 is 14 because it's just 28 a half a time, so 28 + 14 = 42.

*Brandi:* I agree, but I did it a different way. I said that 1 1/2 plus 1/ 1/2 is 3, and so you count by 2s and 3s.

*Mr. B.:* Brandi, can you show us how you counted by 2s and 3s?

*Brandi:* Sure it's like this [writes the numbers 2–28 by 2s and, beneath them in pairs, writes the numbers 3–42 by 3s, as shown in figure 4.15].

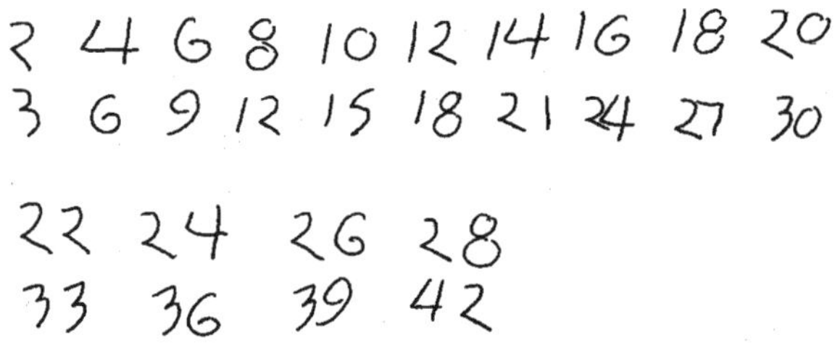

2 4 6 8 10 12 14 16 18 20
3 6 9 12 15 18 21 24 27 30

22 24 26 28
33 36 39 42

Fig. 4.15. Brandi's work to show how she counted by twos and threes to get her answer

*Hillary:* I agree because I kind of did it like Brandi, but I just added them all up [displays her addition work, shown in figure 4.16].

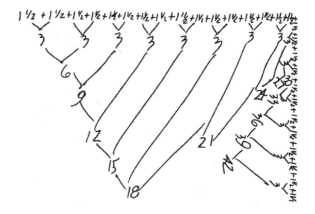

Fig. 4.16. Hillary's work, in which she has "added them all up" to get the same answer, 42, as Brandi and Dallas did

| | |
|---|---|
| *Mr. B.:* | What if each rhombus weighs 2 ounces, how much would the block weigh? |
| *Austin:* | Well, that's 28 + 28 because you just go, "28 × 2" because it is 28 two times. So that's 56. |
| *Mr. B.:* | Fifty-six what? |
| *Austin:* | Fifty-six ounces. |
| *Mr. B.:* | How do you know 28 + 28 equals 56 ounces? |
| *Austin:* | Because 25 + 25 is 50 and 3 + 3 is 6, so it is 56 ounces. |
| *Hillary:* | I agree because 20 + 20 is 40, and 8 is 48, and 8 is 56. |
| *Mr. B.:* | Now let's get back to the rhombi and the block on the balance. If the 28 rhombi balance the block, how many hexagons would balance the block? [The children worked on the problem.] |
| *Brandi:* | It's 9 hexagons because you take, like, 27 (rhombi) because, like, you don't have another one, and you go, "3, 6, 9, 12," and you keep going until you get to 27, and you can only use threes to get to 27 because you want to get up to 27. |
| *Dallas:* | I disagree because it takes 28 rhombus, not 27, to balance the block. |
| *Brandi:* | Yes, but there isn't a 28, because when you count threes, you don't get 28, you get 3, 6, 9, 12, 15, 18, 21, 24, 27, 30, and stuff like that. |
| *Mr. B.:* | Brandi, I think what Dallas is trying to say is that you solved a different problem. You solved a problem with 27 rhombi, and this problem has 28 rhombi. |
| *Brandi:* | "I know, that's why I said you don't have the one, you don't need to count it if you're counting by threes. [At this point Brandi experienced down shifting and was unable to see beyond the mistake she had made. So I decided to have someone else share her or his solution so that Brandi could see the problem from a perspective different from her own.] |
| *Mr. B.:* | Did someone solve this problem using 28 rhombi? |
| *Hillary:* | 9 1/3 hexagons because 3 rhombus make a hexagon, but the 1 more is the same as a third of a hexagon. |
| *Dallas:* | I agree, but like Mr. B. said, it's not "rhombus." |
| *Hillary:* | I don't get it. |
| *Mr. B.:* | What don't you get? |
| *Hillary:* | I don't get what he means, because this is a rhombus. |

| *Dallas:* | It is a rhombus. But like Mr. B. said, when you have more than one of them, you say "rhombi," not "rhombus." You should have said 3 rhombi, not 3 rhombus. |
| --- | --- |
| *Mr. B.:* | Did anyone else solve this problem? |
| *Austin:* | Well, I thought this can't be that hard, so I went, "3, 6, 9, 12, 15, 18, 21, 24, 27," but that's not 28. |
| *Mr. B.:* | Why did you go, "3, 6, 9," and so on? |
| *Austin:* | Because 3 rhombus fit inside a hexagon, so that's why I went, "3, 6, 9, 12," and you just keep going and you get 9 hexagons, but that didn't work, because that's 27, not 28. So I figured that it's going to be a fraction because you only got 1 (rhombus), not the 3 that you need to make a hexagon. So I cut it into 8 pieces [illustrates his approach with a sketch as seen in figure 4.17]. |

Fig. 4.17. Austin's illustration to demonstrate his approach of cutting the hexagonal trapezoid into 8 pieces

## Challenging an incorrect solution strategy

| *Mr. B.:* | Why did you cut the hexagon into 8 pieces? |
| --- | --- |
| *Austin:* | When I cut it (hexagon) in half, that was a trapezoid, and I didn't want a trapezoid, so I cut into fourths and that wasn't right, so I cut it into eighths so it made triangles, and 2 triangles is a rhombus, so it's 9 hexagons and 2/8. |
| *Brandi:* | I disagree because 6 triangles make a hexagon, not 8. |
| *Austin:* | Eight pieces, not 6 triangles. |
| *Mr. B.:* | Brandi, when you say "6 triangles make a hexagon," what do you mean? |
| *Brandi:* | Look, if you take a hexagon, it is the same as 6 triangles if you put them like this [uses 6 triangular pattern blocks to show their equivalence to a hexagonal pattern block]. |

Fig. 4.18. Brandi's block arrangement to show that 6 triangular
pattern blocks are equivalent to 1 hexagonal pattern block

*Austin:* I know that, what I mean, it's 8 pieces.

*Mr. B.:* I think I know what Brandi and Austin are trying to say. I think
we can all agree with Brandi that when you use pattern blocks,
6 triangles are the same as one hexagon (Austin nodded in
agreement). But I also agree and disagree with Austin. I agree that
2 pattern-block triangles make a rhombus, but I would like
everyone to look closely at Austin's drawing and see what you notice
about Austin's pieces.

*Austin:* Oh, now I get it—2 of them don't make a rhombus. I don't know
what they make, but it's not a rhombus [outlines two of the pieces
in his drawing, as shown in figure 4.19].

Fig. 4.19. Austin's modified drawing, in which he outlined two pieces
to illustrate his realization that they do not make a rhombus shape

*Mr. B.:* So two triangles don't always make a rhombus?

*Austin:* Well, they do, but they got to be the right kind of triangles like the
pattern blocks, and these pieces aren't right.

*Dallas:* [Interrupts excitedly] Hey, wait, his way does work, but it's not
2 pieces, it's 3. Look, these 3 pieces make a rhombus, and these
3 pieces make a rhombus, and these pieces make a rhombus
[outlines pieces differently in Austin's drawing, as shown in figure
4.20]. So he has it, but it's not 2/8 like Austin said, it's 3/8.

Fig. 4.20. Dallas's modification of Austin's drawing, outlining different groupings of pieces to support his answer of 3/8

| | |
|---|---|
| *Austin:* | Dallas is right, it does work; I just needed 1 more piece. |
| *Mr. B.:* | I agree with Dallas that 3 of the pieces in Austin's drawing do make a rhombus, but I disagree that the answer is 3/8. To see why I disagree, you are going to have to look even closer at Austin's drawing. |
| *Austin:* | I don't get it. It's 3 out of 8 pieces, so it's 3/8. |
| *Dallas:* | Austin's right, we're not using the regular triangles (pattern blocks), we're using 3 pieces, and they make a rhombus; so it has to be 3/8. [Once again I asked the children to look very closely at the drawing, and they all seemed convinced that 3/8 was correct. Finally, Brandi made a comment.] |
| *Brandi:* | It's not 3/8 because the pieces are not the same size. Look, the ones on the sides are bigger than the ones in the middle, and when you do a fraction, they all have to be the same size. So Austin's way won't work, because the pieces aren't the same. |
| *Mr. B.:* | I agree with Brandi. But I also agree with Dallas that the 3 pieces do make a rhombus, we just don't have a way to write the answer because some of the pieces are larger than some of the other pieces. Can anyone see how much bigger the larger pieces are than the smaller ones? |
| *Austin:* | Oh, I get it, you have to cut the big ones in half, and then they will be the same [altering his drawing to look like figure 4.21]. |

Fig. 4.21. Austin's revised drawing, in which he has made the triangular pieces the same size

> *Austin:* So it's "1, 2, 3, 4" out of "1, 2, 3, 4, 5, 6, 7, 8, 9, 10, 11, 12." So it's [pause] I'm not sure how to say it, I know it is 4 out of 12, but I'm not sure how to say it.
>
> *Dallas:* How do you think you would say it?
>
> *Austin:* "Four twelves" or something.
>
> *Dallas:* That's it, only you say "twelfths," not "twelves."
>
> *Mr. B.:* Austin, so what is your answer?
>
> *Austin:* Nine and 4/12 hexagons.

## Introducing a Minilesson

Because of the children's confusion over the fractional representation of 3/8, I decided to take the activity in a different direction and do a minilesson that would approach the same issue from a different perspective. I knew that the dimensions of a rectangular face of Unit Block C was 1 3/8 × 2 3/4 (or 1 3/8 × 2 6/8) inches, so I asked the children to get rulers and determine the perimeter of that face. This task gave the children a chance to practice their measuring skills and computation skills, as well as presented a different way to represent fractional quantities, using the ruler rather than drawings of "pieces" of pattern-block shapes as the model.

> *Mr. B.:* How did you find the perimeter of the rectangular face of block C?
>
> *Hillary:* Well, first I measured the sides, and they are 1 3/8, and 2 6/8, and 1 3/8, and 2 6/8, and then I added them up and got 8 2/8 inches.
>
> *Mr. B.:* But how did you add the numbers?
>
> *Hillary:* Well, I did it like this: I said [that] 1 + 1 + 2 + 2 is 6 because 2 + 2 is 4 and it's just 2 more, so that's 6 (inches). Then I took 3/8 and 3/8 and that's 6/8 because—you can see it on the ruler when you count three of them, and then just count three more and you get 6/8. Then I took 6/8 and 6/8, and that's 12/8, but that didn't look right because I don't think it can be that way, like, you can't have more than 8/8, because that is 1 inch. So I took 2/8 off of one of them and put it on the other one, and if you count two more (1/8s) on the ruler, that makes 1 inch, and I have 4/8 left on the other one. But I still had the 6/8 from before, so I took another 2/8 off and put it on, and that made another 1 inch. So that's 2 more (inches), so it's 8 inches and the 2/8 that you got left over [illustrates her thinking as shown in figure 4.22].

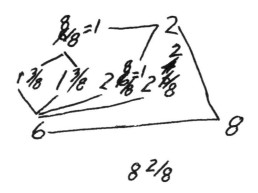

Fig. 4.22. Hillary's work to support her answer of 8 2/8 inches

*Austin:* I agree because I did it the same way, and I agree it is 8 2/8 inches all the way around.

*Mr. B.:* Next I would like you to find the perimeter of the square face on block B. [The dimensions of square face on Unit Block B are 2 3/4 (6/8) × 2 3/4 (6/8) inches. When the children were ready, I asked Dallas to share his solution.]

*Dallas:* Since it is a square, I only needed to measure one side and times it times 4.

*Mr. B.:* Why do you multiply by 4?

*Dallas:* Because there is 4 sides, so you do it 4 times like I said, and that's 2 four times, which is 8, and that's 6/8 four times, which is 24/8, I think, but I'm not sure because like Hillary said, I don't know if you can do it like that. So I'm not sure, but if you can, it's easy because you just count 8/8 and 8/8 and 8/8 and you got it—it's 24/8. So you just count 1, 2, 3 because that's 3 of them (8/8), and 8 from before plus 3 makes 11 inches.

*Hillary:* I agree, but I kind of did it different, but I agree it is 11 inches.

*Mr. B.:* What is the perimeter of a large rectangular face on block A? [The dimensions of that face on Unit Block A are 2 3/4 (or 2 6/8) × 5 1/2 inches. After the children finished solving the problem, I asked Brandi to share first.]

*Brandi:* I did it like Hillary. So I said the inches is 14 because 5 and 5 is 10 and 2 and 2 is 4, so that's 14. And 1/2 and 1/2 is 1, so I just put that aside. And 6/8 and 6/8 is 8/8 and 4/8 because you just move two of them over so it's easier to see what it really is. And that's another 1. So it's 16 and 4/8.

| | |
|---|---|
| *Austin:* | I agree and disagree. Brandi, I agree that it's 16 4/8, but I disagree, you don't move 2, you moved 2/8. |
| *Brandi:* | What do you mean? |
| *Austin:* | You said you move 2 over to the 6/8, but what you really did was move 2/8 over, not 2. |
| *Brandi:* | OK, I get it. |

## Revisiting the Problem

With the minilesson over, we resumed our discussion of the children's solutions for the pattern-block problem: If the 28 rhombi balance the block, how many hexagons would balance the block?

*Comparing solution strategies*

| | |
|---|---|
| *Mr. B.:* | Did anyone solve this problem a different way? |
| *Dallas:* | I put 3 rhombus [pause], I mean rhombi, on a hexagon and counted until I got up to 27, and that made 9 hexagons because "1, 2, 3" is 1 (hexagon) [pause]; "4, 5, 6" is 2 (hexagons) [pause]; "7, 8, 9" is 3 (hexagons); and you just keep going until you get to 27, and you have 9 hexagons. But I still have 1 more rhombus, but if you put it on a hexagon, you can see it is 1/3 because 2 rhombus [pause], I mean rhombi, are missing [displays his work, as seen in figure 4.23]. |

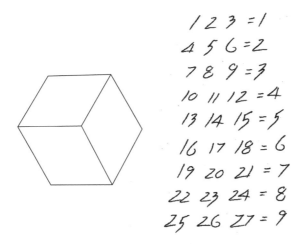

Fig. 4.23. Dallas's work to support his answer of 9 1/3 hexagons

*Mr. B.:*    What do you mean, "2 are missing"?

*Dallas:*    The other 2 rhombi, because they are 2/3 of the hexagon and the 1 that's there is 1/3 of a hexagon [labels his drawing as seen in figure 4.24].

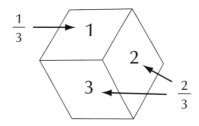

Fig. 4.24. Dallas's drawing as labeled in response to the teacher's inquiry about his statement "2 are missing"

*Austin:*    Hey, that's cool because the 2 and the 3 make 2/3.

*Mr. B.:*    Austin, I'm not sure I understand what you mean?

*Austin:*    The 2 and the 3 on the rhombus, when you put them together, they make 2/3, like, the numbers make 2/3 and the rhombuses make 2/3.

*Mr. B.:*    That is interesting. But look, when you put the numbers 1 and the 3 on the rhombi together, they make 1/3, but when you put the rhombi with these numbers on them together, they are not 2/3s of the shape.

*Austin:*    [Long pause] Hmm, that's weird. I guess it just works sometimes.

## Asking probing questions

*Mr. B.:*    Now I have a new problem. If the 28 rhombi balance the block, how many tapezoids would balance the block? [The children worked on the problem and shared their solutions with their partners. When they were finished, we resumed our discussion.]

*Brandi:*    Well, why I thought it was 18 2/6 is because if we were doing hexagons like we just did, it is 9 1/3 hexagons, so you just have to double it (9 1/3) because it's twice as many, so double 9 is 18 and double 1/3 is 2/6.

*Hillary:*  I agree and disagree. I agree with how you did it, but it's not 2/6. I know how you did this because I used to think the same thing, that you just add them up, but you kind of do, but not the way you did it, because 1/3 + 1/3 is not 2/6, it's 2/3 because when you add them, the answer gets bigger, and 2/6 is not bigger than 1/3 and 1/3.

*Mr. B.:*  Hillary, I'm not sure what you mean when you say "the answer gets bigger" when you add them.

*Hillary:*  When you add two numbers, the answer is bigger than the numbers you are adding, like 6 is bigger than 2 and 4 when you add 2 and 4.

*Mr. B.:*  Brandi, could you show us how you figured out that 1/3 + 1/3 equals 2/6?

*Brandi:*  Well 1/3 + 1/3 is 2/6—you just add them—1 + 1 is 2 and 3 + 3 is 6, so it's 2/6.

*Mr. B.:*  Why did you add the numbers this way?

*Brandi:*  Because my sister showed me how to do it, and she is in middle school.

## Using models

To the reader it might seem strange that previously in this chapter, Brandi was able to correctly find the perimeter of the rectangular face of unit block A, which measures 2 3/4 (6/8) × 5 1/2 inches, yet she could not correctly add 1/3 + 1/3. Brandi's inability to solve similar problems seems to lie in the power of mathematical tools to serve as visual aides—in this instance the power of a ruler to model fractional quantities.

Suspecting that just such a word problem might be on the algebra midterm, Gary came prepared.

Unlike the character in the preceding cartoon, whose use of a model may not lead to a solution of the problem he is trying to solve, Brandi was able to successfully model the fractional quantities in the previous perimeter problem using a ruler. With the aid of the ruler, she was able to *see* the fractions as represented by actual units that she could count and combine. Brandi used the ruler to *think with and about* the problem. The ruler became a tool to organize and clarify her solution process. In contrast, Brandi solved the immediate problem by relying on the misinformation supplied to her by her older sister instead using a tool to model the fractions.

## Requesting clarification

> *Mr. B.:*   Hillary, could you show Brandi why you think it is 2/3 instead of 2/6. [Hillary used the pattern blocks and traced a hexagon shape on her paper. Then she used a rhomboidal pattern block and traced it three times inside the hexagon. She then labeled her drawing as shown in figure 4.25].

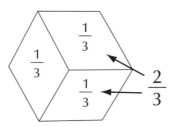

Fig. 4.25. Hillary's drawing, in which she first traced a hexagon shape using the hexagonal pattern block, then traced three rhombi inside the hexagon using the rhomboidal pattern block

> *Hillary:*   See, 1/3 and 1/3 is 2/3 of the hexagon.
>
> *Mr. B.:*   How much is 2/6 of the hexagon? [The children thought about the question.]
>
> *Brandi:*   Oh, I get it, it's a rhombus, just like before when Austin said that 8 triangles make a hexagon and I said that 6 triangles make a hexagon but 2 triangles is a rhombus.
>
> *Mr. B.:*   Brandi, if you double 9 1/3, how much will it equal?
>
> *Brandi:*   18 and 2/3.

*Arriving at agreement*

> *Mr. B.:*   Did anyone solve this problem a different way.
>
> *Dallas:*   What I thought is, 18 and 2/3 trapezoids because 1 1/2 rhombi make a trapezoid; just look at my drawing and you can see it [displays the drawing shown in figure 4.26]. So 1 1/2 + 1 1/2 is 3 rhombi, but that's the same as 2 trapezoids, and I just keep doing that eight more times because 27 rhombi are on the balance. So that's 18 trapezoids, but you got 1 more (rhombus) because you are only up to 27, not 28, and how I know a rhombus is 2/3 of a trapezoid is because if you cut off the triangle, you have 2/3 left. So I think it is 18 and 2/3 of a trapezoid.

Fig. 4.26. Dallas's drawing to support is answer of 18 2/3 trapezoids

> *Austin:*    How did you know that a rhombus is 2/3 of a trapezoid?
>
> *Dallas:*    If you cut a trapezoid into thirds, you get 3 triangles. But remember what Brandi showed you, 2 triangles make a rhombus, so a rhombus is 2/3 of a trapezoid.
>
> *Hillary:*   I agree it's 18 and 2/3, but I said it's 2/3 because 2 triangles is the same as a rhombus and that's what we started with, and 3 triangles is the same as a trapezoid and that's what we are supposed to come up with. So a rhombus is only 2 of the 3 triangles, so it's 2/3 of a trapezoid.
>
> *Mr. B.:*    All of you are wonderful problem solvers.

# Collaboration: The Dance of Learning

Throughout these activities the children used the small-group discussions to generate shared knowledge that was greater than their individual understandings. They were doing more than just cooperating with one another—they were collaborating.

I have often thought that cooperation is like two people walking together but that collaboration is like two people dancing. For me, it was a true joy to watch these children participate in the dance of learning. It is the main reason I continue to teach in spite of the seemingly impossible demands and expectations our society now places on schools and teachers. If someone asked me what I need most as a teacher, I would answer, "time"—time to spend with children, talking about mathematics, listening to their solutions to problems, and joining with them in small discussion groups as they perform a mathematical dance—because "just as music comes alive in the performance of it, the same is true of mathematics" (Devlin 1994, pp. 3–4).

# Looking Back at the Activities

Thus a teacher of mathematics has a great opportunity. If he fills his allotted time with drilling his students in routine operations he kills their interest, hampers their intellectual development, and misuses his opportunity. But if he challenges the curiosity of his students by setting them problems proportionate to their knowledge, and helps them to solve their problems with stimulating questions, he may give them a taste for, and some means of, independent thinking.

—George Pólya
*How to Solve It*

It's not that I'm so smart, it's just that I stay with the problem longer.

—Albert Einstein

IN CONDUCTING small-group discussions similar to those described in chapters 3 and 4 with the rest of the children in the class, some issues arose that may be of interest to others who would like to replicate the activities.

## What the Activities Can Tell Us

To my surprise, what at first appeared to be minor details in the activities later turned out to make a big difference in how the children interpreted and responded to various aspects of the problems they were asked to solve. As shown in the cartoon at the right, *little things* need to be attended to because they can have big consequences.

"Taking care of the little things is a big thing."

## What the Activities Can Tell Us about "Little Things"

### Recording format

The first little thing that made a difference was the type of recording form the children used to keep track of their answers. Originally I planed to use recording form A (fig. 5.1). Then one of the teachers in the school commented that the manner in which the blocks were shown on the form might unintentionally give children clues about how to proceed in solving the problems. I therefore created forms B, C, and D (fig. 5.2).

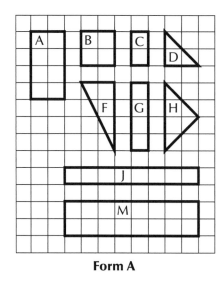

**Form A**

Fig. 5.1. Original recording form

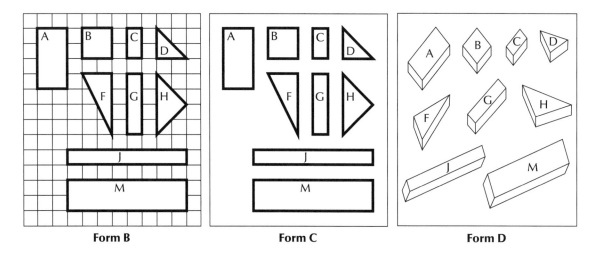

| Form B | Form C | Form D |

Fig. 5.2. Alternative recording forms

Finally I decided to create form E, which had no pictorial information at all (fig. 5.3).

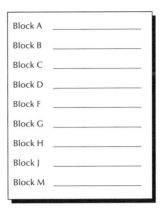

Fig. 5.3. Final recording form, containing no
pictorial information

As one might expect, form A provided the most clues, and children who used that form experienced the highest degree of success when solving problems posed during the activities. In addition to the pictorial clues, form A also furnished an alternative way of solving the problems, as demonstrated by Antonio's use of the grid (fig. 3.42). Form E provided the fewest clues, and children using that form took longer to solve the problems. Forms B, C, and D were somewhat in between the extremes represented by form A and form E. The drawings on the forms seemed to give the children clues as to which face on the block would be most useful when solving the problems. The pictorial representations on forms A, B, C, and D also seemed to suggest to the children that they should use a horizontal orientation of the blocks when solving the problems. A question I plan to explore in the future is whether more children will solve the problems using a vertical orientation of the blocks (as Nicole and 25 percent of her classmates did) if all the blocks are depicted on recording form D in a vertical rather than horizontal position.

## Reference point

The second little thing that made a difference was which of the blocks was on the balance and served as a reference point. If block C was on the balance, the children's preferred strategy was to use doubling or adding to predict the weight of the other blocks. Their predisposition to use that strategy made predicting the weight of block D (the triangular shaped block) problematic because it required them to use a different strategy. In contrast, if block A was on the balance, the children's preferred strategy was to divide the weight of the blocks in half to predict the weight of the other blocks. Their predisposition to use that strategy made predicting the weight of block D fairly simple because they could take one-half of the weight of block B to arrive at the answer.

## Shapes of the blocks

The third little thing that made a difference has already been alluded to previously—the shapes of the blocks themselves. The children could more easily make predictions about the weight of the square-faced or rectangle-faced blocks than of the triangle-faced blocks. That outcome was not surprising, because many children have difficulty arranging the triangle-faced blocks into the shape of one of the other blocks. In contrast, children have little difficulty arranging the square-faced or rectangle-faced blocks to form the shape of another block.

## Order of the problems

The fourth little thing that made a difference was the order in which the children were asked to solve the problems. If block C was on the balance and children were asked to predict weight of block A (before predicting the weight of block B), the task was more challenging than if they first solved for block B and then for block A. The same was true if block A was on the balance and the children solved for block C before solving for block B.

# What the Activities Can Tell Us about Young Children

## Centration

When Melissa (chapter 2) used her "hand balance" to predict the weight of the first block, she displayed one of the common characteristics of young children—called *centration*—the tendency to focus on only one characteristic of an object. In the instance described, Melissa focused totally on the weight of the object and ignored all the other features of the object, especially its size and shape in relation to the block on the balance. She again displayed centration when she ignored the width of a block and focused entirely on its length when making her prediction for the weight of block G (fig. 3.13).

## Egocentrism

In contrast, when Melissa, Nicole, and Nicholas had difficulty understanding Taylor's solution for predicting the weight of block B, they displayed the characteristic of *egocentrism*—the inability to understand another person's point of view. They seemed to be so focused on their way of solving the problem that they could not get outside their own thoughts to explore ideas that were different from their own. Another instance of egocentrism happened when Nicholas, Taylor, and Nicole struggled to understand Melissa's solution for the triangle-faced block D (fig. 3.24).

## Irreversibility

Another characteristic the children in the class displayed was *irreversibility*—the inability to reverse the direction of one's thinking or actions. Lindsey evidenced that trait when her group was asked to find one-half of 4 but Lindsey instead doubled 4, just as she had doubled the other numbers in the mental mathematics exercises leading up to the question that called for halving.

## Inability to conserve

A fourth characteristic common among young children is their *inability to conserve*—that is, their inability to understand that a quantity is fixed even when its physical appearance is changed; thus they base misjudgments on perception rather than logic. An example of this phenomenon occurred when Nicholas and Taylor believed that bock D was bigger than block C because "it just looks bigger." Surprisingly, they remained convinced that block D was bigger than block C even though they agreed with Melissa's solution, which clearly showed that the two blocks were the same size and therefore block D could not be bigger than block C.

## Additional tendencies

Throughout the discussions, the reader may have noticed several other aspects about the children I have described:

- First, they exhibited a tendency to *focus on the surface features of the problems.* Although the children demonstrated a great deal of talent in solving problems, they showed a real inability to identify the mathematical concepts that were embedded within the problems and that formed the foundation for their solutions.

- Second, although their comments at times may have seemed unclear to the reader, the children seemed to have *little difficulty understanding one another.*

- Third, instead of using formal logic to explain their thinking, they often used *nonlogical thinking.* This tendency was demonstrated several times during the discussions, for example, (a) when Nicholas tried to cut the blocks into glue sticks (fig. 3.7), (b) when several of the children attempted to use the *enclosure* method to predict the weight of the triangle-faced blocks (figs. 3.22 and 3.40), and (c) when Zachery tried to predict the weight of block F by standing it upright on block A (fig. 3.43). In addition to using nonlogic, the children sometimes relied on the use of *circular logic.*

**Agnes**
**by T. Cochran**

- Fourth, when crafting their unique and often most interesting solutions to problems, the children seemed to use a process I call *simplistic enlightenment.* Although some of the children skillfully used the blocks or made drawings to show *how* they solved problems, their descriptions of their solution processes were frequently expressed in simplistic, bare-bones terms that were disorganized, unclear, or incomplete. Important steps were left out, and mathematical terms were misused or omitted. In place of words, the children used a great deal of nonverbal communication, and attempted to let the manipulatives or their drawings speak for them.

## What the Activities Can Tell Us about Children's Understanding

In addition, the children's inability to explain *why* they solved problems in distinctive ways was even more elusive, often remaining an unsolved mystery for both themselves and me. From the children's perspective, their individualized solutions to problems just seemed to miraculously appear. When asked why she solved a problem in a particular way, Andrea's response was typical of the way most children would answer that question: "I don't know. I just did it."

### Nourishing children's enlightenment

I am not sure I will ever fully understand the source of children's enlightenment, but I do know that it is a gift that teachers should attempt to nourish in children. As Albert Einstein is said to have observed,

> The intuitive mind is a sacred gift and the rational mind is a faithful servant. We have created a society that honors the servant and has forgotten the gift. (Einstein, 1879–1955).

I suspect, however, that access to the gift of understanding is often the result of nothing more than trying to understand—attempting to make sense of something—and the first step in sense making is to solve problems in ways that makes sense to oneself, then to respond to the feedback one receives from others. Sometimes a single insight that emerges from a child's struggle to make sense of a problem can deepen the child's understanding of a mathematical concept in ways that cannot be achieved by completing hundreds of drill-and-practice exercises.

### Fostering patience and perseverance

THE BORN LOSER® by Art and Chip Sansom

The Born Loser © 1994 Art Sansom. All rights reserved. Rperinted with permission of United Media.

Understanding, however, takes time, and when children say, "I get it," they often don't. Genuine understanding happens in starts and stops, bits and pieces, through trial and error, and usually occurs over extended periods of time as children participate in many different but related activities. In some classrooms, when children are asked to solve challenging problems, they respond with feelings of frustration and anger because they cannot find the answer in a few seconds. As it turns out, little things, such as the *willingness to try* and *not give up*, turn out to be very important when trying to solve challenging problems. Perhaps the source of the children's enlightenment in the preceding chapters is their belief in the idea that mathematics is supposed to make sense and that they can make sense of mathematics if they persist in their pursuit of knowledge. Albert Einstein once said, "It's not that I'm so smart, it's just that I stay with the problem longer." One of the greatest services teachers can perform for children is to help them learn to be patient and perseverant and to keep a positive attitude when learning to be mathematical problem solvers.

## What the Activities Can Tell Us about Children's and Teachers' Roles during Small-Group Discussions

### The children's role

The children played many different roles during the described activities as they constantly shifted between thinking creatively when formulating their solutions to thinking critically about the solutions of others. Likewise, I played many roles as I shifted from problem poser to discussion facilitator. Shifting roles can be challenging for both children and teachers, but with practice all the participants become more comfortable with the discussion process.

Children benefit most from the problem-solving portion of an activity by playing the roles of—

- inquisitive questioner, when they ask clarifying questions if the problem is unclear or terminology is not understood;

- risk taker, when they solve problems in ways that make sense to them; and

- detailed recorder, when they represent all the steps in their solution process.

Children benefit most from collaborative discussions when they play the roles of—

- articulate communicator, by expressing their thoughts in ways that can be understood;

- interested audience, by engaging in active listening; and

- helpful collaborator, by providing constructive feedback to others

### The teacher's role

When the children are solving problems, my main role is to assist them in their efforts to engage in sense making, and I do so primarily by asking clarifying questions. In general, teachers facilitate children's attempts to solve problems when they—

- exercise professional judgment when deciding whether children genuinely need assistance or whether they are better served by simply being left alone to work toward a solution;

- use direct observation to assess children's current level of understanding, then use the information gleaned to shape the discussion and pose appropriate questions;

**113**

- model the use of mathematical terms, and encourage the children to use them as well; and

- give children access to the tools and materials they need to solve problems in ways that make sense to them.

When children discuss their solutions with one another, my primary role is to learn from them. I try to do whatever is required to understand children's thinking, and to help them understand one another as well. I ask *probing* questions, especially if the solution is unclear, incomplete, or contains an error; and I ask *leading* questions to help guide children toward a deeper understanding of the mathematical concepts embedded within problems. As noted in the NCTM's *Principles and Standards for School Mathematics*, "students in the lower grades need help from teachers in order to share mathematical ideas with one another in ways that are clear enough for other students to understand" (NCTM 2000, p. 61).

In general, teachers facilitate children's discussions when they—

- encourage children to give reasons why they agree or disagree with others, and keep discussions focused on children's solution processes rather than the answers to problems;

- seize the teachable moment, and use children's solutions as a springboard to reinforce a mathematical skill or teach a new skill;

- ask probing or leading questions to determine whether children are confident in their solution strategies and whether they can explain all the steps in their solution process clearly and completely;

- model how to ask clarifying questions by using such phrases as "I don't quite understand" or "I'm confused";

- encourage active listening by modeling and emphasizing appropriate listener behaviors: (a) keep your eyes on the speaker; (b) be able to restate what the speaker has said in your own words; and (c) provide feedback to the speaker that is helpful and informative;

- encourage risk taking by showing that you value mistakes as learning opportunities and an unavoidable part of becoming a problem solver.

## The Importance of Small-Group Discussions in the Mathematical Lives of Children

Small-group discussions are especially useful in creating an environment in which children can feel comfortable sharing their solutions and collaborating with peers. Some children are reluctant to share their ideas in front of the whole class, and discussions involving the entire class can be challenging for teachers to orchestrate and manage.

As can be seen from the discussions described, children do make mistakes and errors. The discussions also demonstrate, however, that children can learn from their mistakes and correct them—especially when they are given the chance to work with peers in small discussion groups. Some teachers and parents worry that children's mistakes may lead to bad habits that are difficult to correct. However, the preceding examples demonstrate that misconceptions can be corrected if children receive constructive feedback. Small-group discussions are particularly effective in providing children with prompt and personalized feedback, not only from the teacher but from other children as well.

# 6

# Using a Multi-age Classroom to Enhance Problem Solving
## Learning to Collaborate, Collaborating to Learn

## Lessons from Geese

*Fact:* As each bird flaps its wings, it creates an uplift for the bird following behind it. By flying in a V formation, the whole flock achieves 71 percent greater flying range than if each bird flew alone.

*Lesson:* When children work together, they can do more with less effort.

*Fact:* When the goose in the front of the V gets tired, it falls back into the formation and another one takes its place.

*Lesson:* When children take turns speaking and listening, they share responsibility for keeping conversations interesting and informative.

*Fact:* The geese in the V honk to encourage those up front.

*Lesson:* When children agree or disagree with one another, they need to make sure that what they say is encouraging and helpful.

*Fact:* When a goose gets sick or wounded, two geese drop out of the V and follow him down to the ground to protect him. They stay with him until he is able to fly.

*Lesson:* If children are to have as much sense as a goose, they need to learn to help one another.

(Adapted from "Lessons from Geese" by Arrien [1991])

FREQUENTLY multi-age classes are created in schools for one of two reasons: one reflects a philosophy of teaching based on how children learn; the second relates to an administrative device used to cope with declining student enrollment or classes that are uneven in size. When assigned to teach multi-age classrooms by administrators attempting to balance class size, teachers are often concerned about how they will teach various subject areas—including mathematics. Because many teachers are most familiar with the traditional

117

drill-and-practice approach to mathematics instruction, a multi-age classroom appears to create more work for teachers—managing multiple mathematics curricula, using multiple teacher guides, creating multiple daily lesson plans, reproducing multiple sets of drill-and-practice worksheets, and so on.

# Meeting the Challenges of a Multi-age Classroom

## Customary Pedagogical Approaches

To meet the challenges of teaching in a multi-age classroom, teachers often consider grouping children by ability to create three or more mathematics groups. This arrangement allows for the teacher to work with one group while the other children complete independent drill-and-practice exercises. Other teachers consider using stations at which children choose activities at their grade level. Still other teachers consider a team-teaching approach, with each teacher being responsible for the instruction of one group of children—typically a high, medium or low group.

All such teachers see the multi-age classroom as somewhat of a problem that must be addressed with a corrective action. They fail to realize that the multi-age setting is not a problem—it is one way to *enhance* the teaching of mathematics, by creating an environment that supports and facilitates children's efforts to learn mathematics with a level of understanding rarely achieved in traditional single-grade classrooms.

## An Alternative Philosophy of Mathematics Education

Ten years ago I began teaching a multi-age class (first-second-third grade) after having previously taught a single-grade class. However, unlike teachers who are assigned by an administrator to teach in a multi-age classroom, I chose to make this change on the basis of a philosophy of mathematics education that I have come to endorse—using a drill-and-practice approach is a very difficult way to *teach* children how to solve mathematics problems, but children can *learn* to be problem solvers, especially it they are in the presence of more experienced practitioners who can model appropriate skills, dispositions, and the use of constructive feedback.

A question I am often asked by other teachers is "Which came first, the idea to switch to a multi-age setting or the idea to use a problem-solving approach to teach mathematics?" For me both ideas developed simultaneously—I could envision how the use of an apprentice model in a multi-age setting would enhance and reinforce problem-solving skills and behaviors, and I also realized that a problem-solving approach, with its emphasis on collaboration and communication, would support the overall goals of the multi-age setting.

In my classroom the multi-age structure has been especially beneficial in helping children develop positive dispositions toward problem solving and mathematics in general. Children often seem to acquire attitudes toward mathematics that are based on the company they keep and the feelings and emotions expressed by their peers. Just as younger children in a multi-age classroom pick up mathematical terms and skills used by their older classmates, they also readily adopt positive preferences for the content of all subjects taught in school, including mathematics.

## The Advantages of a Multi-age Classroom

I have found that a multi-age classroom is an especially effective environment for implementing a problem-solving approach to mathematics instruction. As noted in the NCTM's *Principles and Standards for School Mathematics* (2000), the use of a problem-solving approach is important for several reasons (Appendix 2).

Problem solving is more than a collection of skills and procedures that are mastered through drill and practice; rather, the art of problem solving is an ability that develops slowly over time as children acquire the habits, dispositions, and behaviors of successful problem solvers. I have found that one of the best ways for children to acquire the characteristics of problem solvers is to solve problems in the company of more skilled practitioners who can model problem-solving abilities for less skilled novices. Prior to adopting a multi-age setting for instruction, I struggled to successfully implement problem-solving in my single-grade classrooms. But I have found that a multi-age setting nourishes and promotes children's learning in several important ways (Veenman 1995; Trusty and Beckenstein 1996; Gaustad 1997; Gorrell 1998; Russell, Rowe, and Hill 1998; Feldman and Gray 1999):

- The multi-age environment encourages children's *cognitive and social growth,* reduces antisocial behavior, and facilitates the use of research-based instructional practices, such as active learning and an integrated curriculum.

- Children are exposed to *rich and diverse discussions* among classroom members who possess a wide range of academic abilities and communication skills. Children can interact with classmates of different developmental levels. Younger or less able students become more excited about learning and benefit from peers who can offer help and encouragement. Younger children also actively tap older children as resources as they seek to develop skills and acquire knowledge. Older or more capable students raise their own level of understanding of content material as they clarify their thinking while helping others, and gain confidence as they assume leadership roles . In addition, older children actively assert responsibility for younger ones and develop an increasingly sophisticated understanding of that responsibility.

- Because the *curriculum spans several grade levels,* high-achieving or gifted children are not held back to grade-level expectations, and low-achieving children benefit from the assistance they receive from more competent peers.

- A multi-age structure is a more *natural social grouping* than a single-age class, and children can develop relationships with children of a wider age range as well as find others of matching abilities.

**119**

- Older children are afforded a meaningful context in which they can review previously learned material, and younger children *engage in complex activities* they would not initiate on their own.

- The atmosphere is one of *decreased competition and increased cooperation,* both of which are necessary conditions for creative and critical thinking. An atmosphere that places less importance on competition emphasizes personal strengths rather than weaknesses and thus causes students to be less aware of individual differences.

- A multi-age program helps build a *sense of community* among children on the basis of traditions, long-term relationships, and shared knowledge created from common experiences.

- Teachers can use the detailed knowledge they acquire about each child to provide *greater continuity of learning experiences,* thereby allowing children to progress more rapidly. The wider range of ages and abilities in a multi-age classroom discourages misleading age-graded expectations and helps teachers focus on students' individual learning needs. Comparisons with other children are lessened because students are evaluated according to their potential and continuous progress, not in comparison with one another or in relationship to grade-level standards.

- A multi-age approach gives teachers the opportunity to establish long-term relationships with parents because children stay in classrooms for more than one year. This continuity helps to facilitate communication between teachers and parents, and avoids the confusion that parents sometimes experience when their child's new teacher does something differently than the previous year's teacher. As a result, parents come to trust teachers, and children come to feel more secure in school. In addition, the multi-age classroom gives parents the opportunity to build long-term relationships with one another, thereby creating a community of adult helpers who can offer better classroom support.

## Potential Disadvantages of a Multi-age Classroom

Although a multi-age environment has its advantages, it also poses potential disadvantages (Miller 1991; Gutierrez and Slavin 1992; Mason and Burns 1996; Russell, Rowe, and Hill, 1998):

- Teachers can tend to present fewer challenges for older students. To minimize that effect, I use a curriculum based on continuous progress for each child.

- Some younger children may experience feelings of inadequacy based on their inability to compete with older children. In fact, I have found that competition between children is actually reduced in a multi-age setting.

- Some younger children may be frustrated by the perceived gap between their work and that of older children, especially if they are very competitive. I have found that this problem can occur in both single-grade and multi-age classrooms, because the cause of the frustration is often the result of some children's inability to achieve perfection in their work and not the result of comparing their work with that of others.

- Some children may be uncomfortable with the fact that the teacher does not treat all children the same way. In fact, I have found the opposite to be true—children in single-grade classrooms are more sensitive to being treated differently, whereas in multi-age classrooms, differences in instruction or teacher expectations are more readily accepted.

- Older children may exhibit disruptive behavior that may be picked up by younger children. To counter this possible problem, older children can be given leadership opportunities, so that instead of adopting negative behaviors, many younger children will strive to emulate their older peers in socially and academically positive ways.

- By staying with one teacher for several years, children may suffer from a teacher's area of instructional weakness, just as they may benefit from a teacher's strengths. To address this problem, teachers should actively engage in ongoing professional development.

- Children can get locked into roles. My experience has shown that this problem is no more severe in multi-age classrooms than single-grade classrooms. However, in multi-age classrooms, older children who are performing academically below their peers have numerous opportunities to assist younger children and gain a sense of personal satisfaction that comes from helping others. In contrast, low-performing children in single-grade classrooms rarely get a chance to assist others.

- Some children may experience a difficult transition when they leave a multi-age classroom and enter a more traditional setting. In fact, I have found that all children experience some difficulty adjusting to a new classroom and teacher, and the problem is no more severe for children when they transition from multi-age classrooms than from single-grade classrooms. Additionally, children in single-grade classrooms must undergo such a transitional process every year, whereas children in multi-age classrooms do not undergo any transition during the years they remain in the multi-age setting.

- Teachers must do more work in planning instruction. Multi-age teaching is not for everyone; it requires a dedicated, motivated, and knowledgeable teacher to do it well and with confidence. However, the beneficial outcomes more than make up for any extra effort required on the part of the teacher.

By being aware of these potential drawbacks, I have found that teachers can avoid them with careful planning and monitoring.

## A Classroom Model for Problem Solving

Although I have used the share-and-compare model (Buschman 2003) for mathematics instruction in both single-grade and multi-age classrooms, the benefits of this model are enhanced when used in a multi-age setting. The model is designed to meet the goal of the NCTM's *Principles and Standards for School Mathematics* to build "a community of learners, where students exchange mathematical ideas not only with the teacher but also with one another" (NCTM 2000, p. 131). The share-and-compare model is more than a tool for learning how to solve problems. It is an ongoing dialog that children use to learn mathematics with confidence and understanding. As noted in the NCTM's *Standards*, "Students who have opportunities, encouragement, and support for speaking, writing, reading, and listening in mathematics classes reap dual benefits: they communicate to learn mathematics, and they learn to communicate mathematically" (NCTM 2000, p. 60).

## Support for Problem-Solving Skills and Dispositions

Although a multi-age classroom does not offer a quick fix to the challenges of teaching problem solving in mathematics, it does offer a setting that supports and facilitates children's efforts to acquire the skills, dispositions, and behaviors of successful problem solvers. As described in chapter 2, at the center of the share-and-compare model are four core beliefs (fig. 6.1) and five core practices (fig. 6.2) (Buschman 2003).

---

### Core Beliefs of the Share-and-Compare Model

- Mathematics is primarily a sense-making activity. Children can learn to make sense of mathematics through problem solving.

- Children can learn how to become problem solvers by participating in a learning community whose members solve problems in ways that makes sense to them, share solutions, and provide one another with useful feedback.

- Children can learn how to be members of a problem-solving community through reflection, sef-assessment, and the gradual acquisition of the dispositions of good problem solvers: patience, persevereance, positive attitude, flexibility, and fluency.

- Children can learn reflection, self-assessment, and the dispositions of good problem solvers through a balanced assessment program that includes direct observation; interviews; scoring guides, or rubrics, and portfolios.

Adapted from Bushman (2003, p. 6)

---

Fig. 6.1. The core beliefs of the share-and-compare model

---

**Core Practices of the
Share-and-Compare Model**

- Children solve challenging problems in ways that makes sense to them. "At all grade levels, students should see and expect that mathematics makes sense" (NCTM 2000, p. 56).

- Children share their solutions with partners. "Students need opportunities to test their ideas on the basis of shared knowledge in the mathematical community of the classroom to see whether they can be understood and if they are sufficiently convincing" (NCTM 2000, p. 61).

- Children tell why they agree or disagree with their partner's solutions.

    From children's earliest experiences with mathematics, it is important to help them understand that assertions should always have reasons. Questions such as "Why do you think it is true?" and "Does anyone think the answer is different, and why do you thinks so?" help students see that statements need to be supported or refuted by evidence.
    (NCTM 2000, p. 56)

- Children share their solutions in small groups and receive feedback in the form of questions or comments.

    Through communication, ideas become objects of reflection, refinement, discussion, and amendment. The communication process also helps build meaning and permanence for ideas and makes them public.
    (NCTM 2000, p. 60)

- Children compare several solutions. "Converstions in which mathematical ideas are explored from multiple perspectives help the participants sharpen their thinking and make connections" (NCTM 2000, p. 60).

Adapted from Bushman (2003, p. 6)

Fig. 6.2. The core practices of the share-and-compare model

When the share-and-compare method is used in a multi-age classroom, the following positive outcomes occur:

- Emergent problem solvers experience a process that allows them to gradually acquire mathematical skills and knowledge with confidence and understanding as they become members of the classroom mathematics community.

123

- Beginning problem solvers engage in activities that allow them to slowly acquire the social skills necessary for working cooperatively and collaboratively with others who represent a wide range of ability levels.

- Younger children participate in projects that promote the development of problem-solving dispositions, which often cannot be modeled by peers in single-grade classrooms, for example, using mistakes as learning tools, taking risks, applying reason and logic, and exhibiting patience and perseverance.

- Younger children benefit from the mentoring provided by their older partners, and older children are challenged to use all their skills as mathematicians, for they soon discover the truth in the saying "You never fully understand something until you try to explain it to someone else."

## Pacing of instruction

Problem-solving methods, such as the share-and-compare model, seem to work best when teachers practice patience by not trying to teach children too much too fast—a common tendency in many single-grade classrooms structured around grade-level expectations. To be successful problem solvers, children must acquire a working knowledge of numerous mathematics terms, conventions, and skills. To digest this much information requires a great deal of time and assistance, and the one thing that teachers in single-grade classrooms seem to lack is the time needed to assist all children in the classroom. However, in a multi-age setting, many student helpers can assist the classroom teacher by providing help to young learners through peer coaching and peer collaboration.

## Appreciation for others' ideas

Also, models for teaching problem solving are most productive when children can see that others value their efforts, even when their best efforts result in incorrect answers. I have found that children in a multi-age classroom come to value the ideas of their classmates, and they are often more appreciative of compliments and comments made by older classmates than those made by the teacher.

## Views of mathematics

When young children in multi-age classrooms share and compare their personal solutions to problems, whether through whole-class discourse, small-group discussions, or conversations with individual partners, they begin to develop views of mathematics and of themselves as mathematicians that are fundamentally different from those held by children in single-grade classrooms. Rather than view mathematics as the memorization of meaningless facts and computational procedures, children in multi-age classrooms begin to see that mathematics can and does make sense as they—

- practice decision making under the guidance of more knowledgeable decision-makers,

- engage in risk taking with the help of more experienced risk-takers, and

- work to make sense of concepts and ideas in the company of more skilled sense-makers.

## Views of classmates as collaborators

In addition, when children have frequent opportunities to solve problems collaboratively, they develop very different relationships with their classmates. In fact, they start to view the other children in the classroom as collaborators, and to perceive the leaning process as a social endeavor rather than an individual struggle. As children share their thinking and compare their work with that of peers who can offer alternative solutions to problems, they not only engage in a conversation with others but also engage in a conversation with their own minds. Two of the most important things in building expertise in children as problem solvers are (a) having the opportunity to see how more experienced classmates solve problems and (b) receiving feedback on their own solution from more knowledgeable peers. Problem solving is not just a collection of skills that are memorized and practiced. It is a craft that requires a certain level of creativity and inventiveness that can be developed slowly over time as one works in the company of more skilled practitioners.

## Why the Apprenticeship Model Works

### Social and psychological support

The social and psychological support fostered in a multi-age classroom creates an emotionally healthy atmosphere that promotes "children's friendships and provide[s] extended contact with adults and peers of varying ages" (Pratt 1983, p. 114). In addition, multi-age classrooms provide an opportunity for "social and academic continuity" (Miller 1995, p. 94). Also, in single-grade classrooms, significant normative pressures are exerted on the children and the teacher to expect all the children to possess the same knowledge and skills. Such pressures lead to a tendency to penalize children who fail to meet grade-level expectations, even though the expectation that all children will learn the same things, in the same way, and at the same time is unrealistic. In contrast, the wider age span in multi-age classrooms results in greater level of acceptance of behavior and performance by teachers as well as by the children themselves.

### Cooperative learning techniques

The cooperative learning techniques that children use when they interact with classmates (e.g., peer coaching and cross-age mentoring) help children develop academic skills as well as positive social behaviors (Blumfed, Marx, Soloway, and Krajcik 1996; Cesarone 1996; Rekurt 1994; Slavin 1991). Although much of children's learning is self-directed, older children and teachers play a major role in guiding children's intellectual development. More capable peers not only extend children's current knowledge but also model a process of acquiring knowledge (Newman, Griffin, and Cole 1989; Rogoff 1990).

### The cultural component of learning

The social component of learning that is embedded in the multi-age model reflects the idea that knowledge is constructed through social interaction in the context of authentic activities

**125**

(Vygotsky 1962). Culture, including the culture of the classroom, has a powerful effect on children's development, and children's language is the primary tool for that development (Moll and Whitmore 1993; Vygotsky 1962). Because what children can do on their own differs from what they can do with help in a multi-age setting, peers can facilitate children's learning through the use of scaffolding techniques within the learners' zone of proximal development (Rogoff and Wertsch 1984; Vygotsky 1962). In addition, the classroom social norms (e.g., respecting the ideas of others, valuing the search for understanding, and experiencing the freedom to make mistakes) that are emphasized in collaborative work enhance children's learning (Brown and Campione 1994; Cobb, Yackel, and Wood 1992).

## The Social Dimension of the Apprenticeship Model

I never expected that the use of a multi-age approach could have such a dramatic effect on the academic and social lives of children. However, I gradually came to realize that the apprenticeship model I had developed for mathematics instruction was not only effective in helping children acquire competence as problem solvers but also useful in promoting the social development of children. Somehow in our efforts to reform schools, we seem to have lost sight of the fact that schools are primarily about giving of oneself in the service of others. Teachers are not the only ones who can practice *giving* in the classroom—older children can give of their time and expertise by mentoring younger children in the acquisition of important skills, attitudes, and behaviors.

One does not have to look very far to see that the social dimensions of education are disappearing as the school curriculum is transformed into a job-training program to prepare children for their role in the global economy. The dog-eat-dog practices of the business world are now mirrored in our schools as schools adopt high-stakes tests, attempt to increase student productivity, and hold children and teachers accountable for achieving annual high performance goals. But often missing from the current dialog on school reform is a call for children to learn how to be members of a community who can collaborate as well as compete, who can discuss as well as debate, who can give as well as take. In our multi-age classroom, the apprenticeship process has become more than a technique for learning mathematics; it has also become a way of learning how to deepen one's own understanding of mathematics in the company of others, and to use the power of relationships to grow academically and socially.

Although several authors have recommended the use of a problem-centered approach to mathematics instruction, none have recognized the importance of an apprenticeship model in supporting children's efforts to become problem solvers in mathematics. A multi-age environment not only supports children's social development but also helps them learn mathematics with understanding as they listen to their classmates' ideas, explore mathematical discoveries, and discuss the big ideas that form the foundation of the mathematics curriculum.

# Developmental Stages of
# Young Problem Solvers
## Learning to Understand, Understanding to Learn

I'm not very big, but I'll do my best.

> I think I can,
> I think I can,
> I think I can.

—Watty Piper, *The Little Engine That Could*

OVER the past ten years, I have attempted to identify the characteristics of young children as they grow and mature as problem solvers in a multi-age (first-second-third-grade) classroom. Teaching in a multi-age classroom has given me the opportunity to observe children over a three-year period and to document their progress using various types of assessment. I *observed* children while they were engaged in the acts of solving problems and sharing solutions with others. I *interviewed* children as they solved problems, and I *scored* children's written work using a scoring guide (rubric).

In this chapter I describe seven stages in the development of young children (see fig. 7.1). An awareness of these stages has helped me develop more realistic expectations of children and turn solving problems into more positive experiences for them. As I examined children's solutions to problems, I became acutely aware of major differences in the way children and adults think and express their thoughts. An awareness of those differences helped me shift my focus toward what children *can* do and away from what they *cannot* do.

Although I present the seven stages in a linear manner, not all children develop problem-solving abilities in a linear fashion. Also, my experience has been that children do not always display all the characteristics of a particular stage when solving a given problem. As Graves and Stuart have noted, "If there is one rule that applies to every child, it is that progress is uneven. Children never follow any series of stages exactly, and sometimes appear to be regressing in one area as they advance in another" (Graves and Stuart 1985, p.169). Therefore, the stages described in this article should be viewed as flexible guidelines.

| **Seven Stages in the Development of Young Problem Solvers** | | |
|---|---|---|
| **Concrete Stage** | | |

❑ *Process:* Children use sense organs and "real" objects. For them, touching is believing.

❑ *Product:* Children display solutions using actual objects represented in the problem.

❑ *Communication:* Communication is usually nonverbal. Children use the real objects to speak for them (they "show" you the answer).

❑ *Reasoning:* Children's thinking is characterized by unconscious incompetence. Children do not know whether they have actually solved the problem (they seem to believe, "What you see is what you get").

**Readiness Stage**

❑ *Process:* Children use a mental set to get ready for and carry out tasks, and they can use fingers as substitutes for real objects.

❑ *Product:* Children display solutions using fingers and naming the quantity represented.

❑ *Communication:* Children's communication is frequently limited to simply stating the answer.

❑ *Reasoning:* Children may use circular logic, that is, restate the problem and the answer as if nothing occurs in between.

**Copying Stage**

❑ *Process:* Children use imitation of others but may begin to attempt trial-and-error solutions.

❑ *Product:* Children can display their solutions using traditional classroom manipulatives. However, they often attempt to use a single manipulative to solve all problems.

❑ Communication: Children's communication is primarily nonverbal, but they can represent their solutions using manipulatives.

❑ *Reasoning:* Children continue to use circular logic, giving obscure reasons for why the solution is correct.

Fig. 7.1. Seven stages in the development of young problem solvers: flexible guidelines

## Mechanical Stage

❑ *Process:* Children use the same habitual response over and over in an attempt to solve all problems in a similar manner.

❑ *Product:* For the first time, children do not need a concrete object but can represent solutions using a drawing. However, their drawings must be exact.

❑ *Communication:* Their communication remains primarily nonverbal, but now children can show how they found the answer using a drawing.

❑ *Reasoning:* Children's circular logic becomes quite formalized and complex. Their thinking is characterized by conscious incompetence, that is, they are aware of their errors but often cannot "see beyond them" because they are determined to use the same strategy over and over.

## Novice Problem Solver

❑ *Process:* Children are beginning to use past experiences to solve new problems, but only if they recognize the new problem as being "similar" to a previously solved problem.

❑ *Product:* Children display their solutions using a variety of methods: drawings, manipulatives, and so on.

❑ *Communication:* Children can now show and tell: they can describe their solution process using drawings and can orally describe the steps used to arrive at the answer.

❑ *Reasoning:* Children's thinking is characterized by unconscious competence; that is, they can solve problems in creative ways but are unable to describe the logic that leads to the correct answer.

## Apprentice Problem Solver

❑ *Process:* Children can modify solutions to previously solved problems to fit new problems.

❑ *Product:* Children usually represent their solutions using abstract drawings instead of manipulatives.

❑ *Communication:* Children begin to use the written description of their solution as a tool to make their thoughts clear to others and to themselves. Their written descriptions often contain appropriate mathematical terminology and include some but not all steps in the solution process.

❑ *Reasoning:* Formal logic has now replaced circular logic. In fact, children are baffled by the circular logic used by other children.

*(Continued)*

---

### Problem Solver

❑ *Process:* Children create "personal" or new solutions for a wide range of problems.

❑ *Product:* Children represent their solutions using abstract symbols (e.g., tally marks, number sentences).

❑ *Communication:* Children can completely describe their solution process by including all the steps used to arrive at an answer. They can often solve the problems in more than one way.

❑ *Reasoning:* Children's thinking is characterized by conscious competence, that is, they know why their solution works, and they can explain their logic to others.

---

## Seven Stages in the Development of Young Problem Solvers

By combining my classroom observations with student interviews and scored work samples, I have identified seven stages in the development of beginning problem solvers (see fig. 7.1).

The following descriptions of each stage of development in becoming a problem solver include examples of children's problem-solving behaviors as detailed in chapters 3 and 4. Also, to help the reader better understand the seven stages, I have included examples of children's solutions for the word problem that follows. I chose the trading-card problem because it is more typical of the kind of word problem used in most classrooms than the blocks problems in chapters 3 and 4.

### The Trading-Card Problem

There are 5 trading cards in each package. Mr. B. wants to give everyone in the classroom 2 cards. How many packages does he need to buy? [Note: On the day the children solved this problem, twenty-five children were present.]

### Concrete Stage

Children at the concrete stage use sense organs and real objects when solving problems. For them, touching is believing, and they must be able to touch real objects to arrive at a solution to the problem. They display their solutions using actual objects represented in the problem. If the problem is about apples, children at this stage will ask for some apples so they can solve the problem. Their communication is usually nonverbal. They use the real objects to speak for them, believing that the objects show the answer. At the concrete stage, children's thinking is characterized by unconscious incompetence—that is, they do not know whether they have actually solved the problem. Rather, they seem to operate under the "What you see is what you get" principle.

## The example of Melissa

An example of a child who exhibited the characteristics of a student at the concrete stage is Melissa. When Melissa used her hands to compare the weight of two objects by pretending to be a "human balance," she showed her need to solve problems using real objects. Although her reasoning process was somewhat creative and her estimate of the weight of the block using her hand balance was reasonable, she admitted, "I don't really know if the answer is correct." This statement reveals a level of *unconscious incompetence* that is typical of children at this stage. Although Melissa displayed the characteristics of more advanced stages of development at the end of the activity, she solved most of the problems described in chapter 3 (as well as additional problems posed during other classroom activities) using real objects.

## Storm's solution

Another example of a child at the concrete stage of development is Storm. Her solution for the trading-card problem on the preceding page is typical of children at this stage of development. Storm solved this problem using a real deck of cards. She counted out five cards and wrapped them in a piece of paper that she glued shut so the cards "would not fall out." She repeated this process until she had made several "packages." Next she walked to the front of the classroom and asked all the children to "Please sit down so I can count you." Then Storm passed out the cards by giving some children two cards and some children one card along with the empty wrapper from the packages. Although several children tried to tell Storm that she had given some children only one card, she ignored their comments. Once all the children had "their" cards, Storm proceeded to give a second card to all the children having only one card. When she was finished, she walked around the room, gathered up all the "empty" wrappers, counted them, and announced that the answer was "ten wrappers."

As one looks at Storm's solution, one can see that she used a common problem-solving strategy called *act it out.* However, Storm had not been taught that strategy, nor did she even know its name; instead, she developed a version of the strategy on her own. Another important aspect of Storm's solution is that she used real objects to solve the problem. Children at the concrete stage are so "concrete" that they often need to use actual objects and directly model the actions described in the problem to arrive at a solution.

Storm documented her solution in the manner shown in figure 7.2. Notice that her written

(I counted them up)

Fig. 7.2. An example of a concrete-stage problem solver's response to the trading-card problem

record did not actually answer the original question stated in the problem. Instead, she very briefly told what she did and seemed to see no reason to record the answer. Storm's response is typical of children at the concrete stage—they will solve a problem, say the answer, and then fail to write the answer on their paper.

## Readiness Stage

During the readiness stage, children use a mental set to get ready for, and carry out, tasks. Their communication is frequently limited to simply stating the answer. Most disconcerting to adults is that children at this stage may use circular logic—that is, restate the problem and the answer as if nothing occurs in between. But most important, children at this stage can use their fingers as substitutes for real objects. They generally display their solutions using fingers and naming the quantity represented.

### The examples of Nicholas and Lindsey

Throughout chapter 3 Nicholas frequently displayed many of the characteristics of a child at the readiness stage. During the activities, he used his fingers as a tool to add or subtract quantities. His communication with others was limited to naming the answer, "I think two." "No, wait, I went 'one glue stick, two glue stick, three glue stick.'" "Well, I agree it's four." His reasoning process was characterized by circular logic, and when asked about his answer, he stated, "I just know (be)cause when you cut it, you get three glue sticks." Another child at this stage was Lindsey, who relied on her fingers to perform routine calculations, such as finding the number that is twice 6.

THE FAMILY CIRCUS — By Bil Keane

"I can't tell you 'cause I'm wearin' my mittens."

### Jacob's solution

An example of a child's solution for the trading-card problem that is representative of the readiness stage is Jacob's solution. Jacob counted the children in the room twice using his fingers as a counting tool. Next he added 25 and 25 by using his fingers to count-on from 25. When he reached fifty, he stopped, and wrote 05 (a transposition of 50) on his paper. Next he began a new counting procedure by raising one finger on his right hand each time he counted to five on his left hand. As he raised each finger on his right hand, he said, "That's one (package)," "That's two (packages)," and so on. Also, each time he lowered the fingers on his left hand, he resumed counting from where he had left off. He continued this process until he reached fifty. At that point he said, "That's ten." He wrote 10 on his paper and said, "I think it's ten."

Jacob took advantage of a manipulative that is easy to use and readily available—his fingers. He adeptly used his fingers to keep track of his counting procedure. This capability marks a real developmental step in his ability to represent objects in an abstract manner. Although he correctly answered the question posed in the original problem, the reader must infer a great deal about his solution process from the response recorded on his paper (see fig. 7.3.). For that reason, directly observing children at the readiness stage while they are solving problems is sometimes beneficial for teachers so that they can note the children's problem-solving processes.

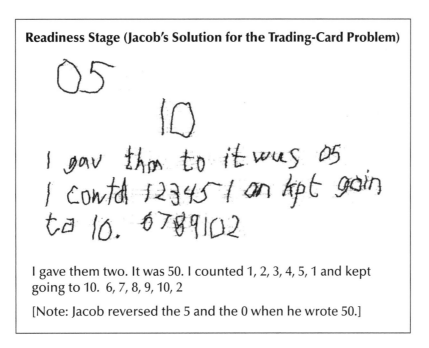

**Readiness Stage (Jacob's Solution for the Trading-Card Problem)**

I gave them two. It was 50. I counted 1, 2, 3, 4, 5, 1 and kept going to 10. 6, 7, 8, 9, 10, 2

[Note: Jacob reversed the 5 and the 0 when he wrote 50.]

Fig. 7.3. An example of a concrete-stage problem solver's response to the trading-card problem

## Copying Stage

At this stage children's problem-solving behavior is characterized by the imitation of others, but on occasion they may begin to attempt trial-and-error solutions on their own if they can make sense of what the problem is asking them to do. They are able to display solutions to problems using traditional classroom manipulatives but often attempt to use a single, favorite manipulative to solve all problems. Their communication continues to be primarily nonverbal. At this stage children continue to use circular logic, but they now make a limited attempt to justify the correctness of their answer with obscure reasons that seem to make little or no sense to anyone else.

### The example of Zachery

During the activities described in chapter 3, Zachery displayed the characteristics of a child at the copying stage of his development. He initially attempted to solve problems by imitating others, then later attempted to solve problems using a trial-and-error approach. His explanations for how he solved each problem relied primarily on the use of the manipulatives to speak for him.

## *Chloe's solution*

Chloe, a child at the coping stage, solved the trading-card problem by using an elaborate procedure of counting and moving tiles around on her desk, as shown in figure 7.4. First, Chloe established a base line of twenty five tiles on her desk. Next she placed two tiles under each base-line tile. Then she paused for a long time as she studied the tiles on her desk. Finally, she counted five of the tiles that were below the base-line tiles and placed them in a stack. Then she took one of the tiles from the base line and placed it on top of the stack. She repeated this process nine times. Then she counted the stacks and said, "I think it is ten."

Children who are at the copying stage usually use traditional classroom manipulatives to keep track of complex mental operations. Although Chloe performed an unusual action by placing tiles from the base line on each of her stacks, she did solve the problem correctly. Additionally, Chloe tended to let the manipulatives speak for her, and therefore her written description lacks many of the steps in her solution process (see fig. 7.4).

## Mechanical Stage

Children who are at the mechanical stage have a tendency to use the same habitual response over and over in an attempt to solve all problems in a similar manner. At this stage children make a big step toward becoming accomplished problem solvers—they can for the first time solve problems without needing to use concrete objects or fingers and instead use a drawing. However, the drawing must be exact. This progress is significant because the use of a drawing creates a permanent record of the solution process. Children's communication remains primarily nonverbal, but now they can *show* how they found the answer using a drawing of what they have done. Their circular logic becomes quite formalized and complex. Their thinking is characterized by conscious incompetence—that is, they are aware of their errors but often cannot see beyond them because they are determined to use the same strategy over and over.

### *The example of Nicole*

In chapter 3 Nicole displayed most of the characteristics of a child at the mechanical stage—she attempted to solve all problems in a similar manner, her communication was primarily nonverbal, she demonstrated lack of flexibility to think about the problems in new ways, and although she was aware of her errors, she struggled to modify her problem-solving strategies and to correct her errors in logic. Although she did not use drawings to solve the problems discussed in chapter 3, on other occasions she used that approach with problems that called for a paper-and-pencil type of solution.

### *Todd's solution*

An example of a solution for the trading-card problem that is representative of the mechanical stage is Todd's solution (see fig. 7.5), which contains one of the most common features of this stage—an exact drawing.

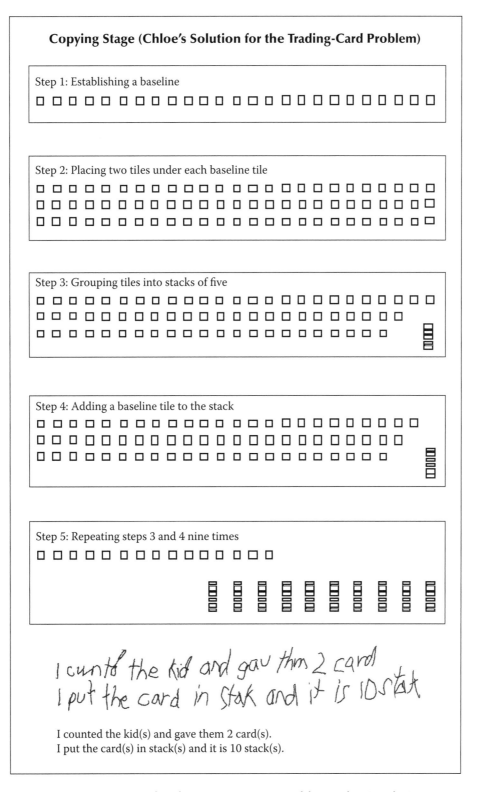

Fig. 7.4. An example of a copying-stage problem solver's solution to the trading-card problem

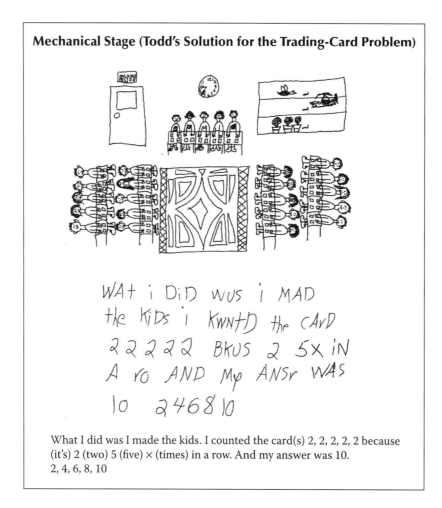

**Mechanical Stage (Todd's Solution for the Trading-Card Problem)**

WAt i DiD wus i MAD
the KiDs i KWNtD the CArD
2 2 2 2 2 BKUS 2 5x iN
A ro AND Mp ANSr WAS
10    2 4 6 8 10

What I did was I made the kids. I counted the card(s) 2, 2, 2, 2, 2 because
(it's) 2 (two) 5 (five) × (times) in a row. And my answer was 10.
2, 4, 6, 8, 10

Fig. 7.5. An example of a mechanical-stage problem solver's solution
to the trading-card problem

Children at this stage seem to reflect a need for *realism* that is similar to that of children at the concrete stage. Just as children progress from using real objects at the concrete stage to later using manipulatives to represent objects, children at the mechanical stage seem to progress from using realistic drawings of objects to later using more abstract representations, such as tally marks or number sentences.

However, an even more important feature of the mechanical stage is that for the first time, children have a genuine, written record of what they have done, which they can examine, discuss with others, and reflect on. Unfortunately, their written record may be incomplete and misleading, as in the instance of Todd's solution. When I first looked at his solution, I could not determine whether Todd had actually solved the problem or whether he had arrived at the right answer by coincidence. His written description seemed to indicate one of two possibilities—the answer was 10 cards because 2 cards were given to 5 children in a row, or the answer was 10 packages because 2 packages of cards were used in each of 5 rows. I asked

Todd how he had solved the problem, and he said, "Well, it's five 2s in a row," and he pointed to the children in one row and counted, "2, 4, 6, 8, 10." Then he said, "So that's 2 packages in a row (be)cause that's 10 cards. So it's 2 five times (be)cause there is five rows, and so that's 2, 4, 6, 8, 10. So it's 10 packages, just like it says" (referring to the answer on his paper). Even when children provide a written description of their solution to a problem, talking with them about their solution is often necessary to facilitate understanding of their thinking.

## Novice Problem Solver

Children who are at the novice problem-solving stage are beginning to use past experiences to solve new problems, but only if they recognize the new problems as being *similar to* previously solved problems. They display solutions to problems using a variety of methods: drawings, manipulatives, and so on. At this stage children take another big step toward becoming better problem solvers in that they can now *show and tell*—that is, they can represent their solution process using drawings, and they can describe the steps used to arrive at the answer. Their thinking is characterized by *unconscious competence*. Children can solve problems in creative ways, and although they can list the steps they used to arrive at the answer, they are unable to describe the logic that lies behind the solution process that leads to the correct answer.

### The examples of Taylor, Andrea, and Jonathan

The children who were at the novice stage in their approach to solving the problems described in chapters 3 and 4 were Taylor, Andrea , and Jonathan. Although each one occasionally displayed one or more of the characteristics of another stage, they solved most problems in ways characteristic of novice problem solvers. For example, Taylor showed some indication of problem-solving behaviors typical of a child at the apprentice stage when he modified his solution strategy for a new problem (finding the number of glue sticks needed to balance block A), and he even displayed some characteristics of the problem-solver stage when he solved that problem in more than one way. But in general, Taylor exhibited the behaviors typical of a child at the novice stage—he was able to *show* how he solved the problems using the blocks to model his solution process, he was able to provide an oral commentary to *tell* what he had done, but he had difficulty abandoning his misconceptions even in the face of clear evidence that refuted them.

### Darlene's solution

An example of a novice problem solver's solution to the trading-card problem is shown in figure 7.6. Although the solution gives the appearance of a well-conceived plan at a more advanced level, it was not Darlene's first attempt at solving the problem. She tired to solve the problem in three different ways before she found the solution method that would "work."

In solving the trading-card problem, Darlene displayed several of the characteristics of the novice stage—she exhibited persistence, her drawing was *not* an exact representation of real objects, and she used various symbols in creative ways to arrive at the correct answer. She was able to depict the *connecting path* in her solution through a combination of pictures, symbols, and words. The reader does not have to infer how she arrived at the answer, even though the written description of her solution process is brief and sketchy.

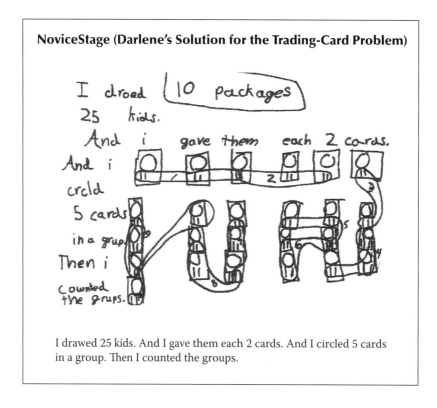

**NoviceStage (Darlene's Solution for the Trading-Card Problem)**

I drawed 25 kids. And I gave them each 2 cards. And I circled 5 cards in a group. Then I counted the groups.

Fig. 7.6. An example of a novice problem solver's solution to the trading-card problem

## Apprentice Problem Solver

At the *apprentice* stage children can routinely modify solutions to previously solved problems to fit new problems. They usually represent their solutions to problems using abstract drawings instead of manipulatives. Children begin to use written descriptions of their solutions as tools to make their thoughts clear to others and to themselves; their written descriptions often contain appropriate mathematical terminology and include some but not all the steps in the solution process. At this stage children take their next big step toward becoming successful problem solvers by replacing circular logic with formal logic. In fact, children at this stage are now baffled by the circular logic used by other children.

### *The examples of Antonio, Austin, Brandi, and Hillary*

Examples of children at the apprentice problem-solving stage in chapters 3 and 4 included Antonio, Austin, Brandi, and Hillary. Throughout the activities, those children frequently modified their solution processes to adjust to the requirements of new problems, and they were adept at using drawings to help others *see* how they arrived at their answers. But most important, they replaced circular logic with formal logic that could be understood by others because it was complete in its analysis of the problem and the mathematical principles that form the basis of the problem-solving strategies they used.

*Chris's solution*

An example of a solution for the trading-card problem that is typical of the apprentice problem-solving stage is Chris's solution, shown in figure 7.7. Chris verified his answer using a second drawing, and the description of what he did included the steps he took to arrive at an answer. In addition, he used the term *because* to justify his actions.

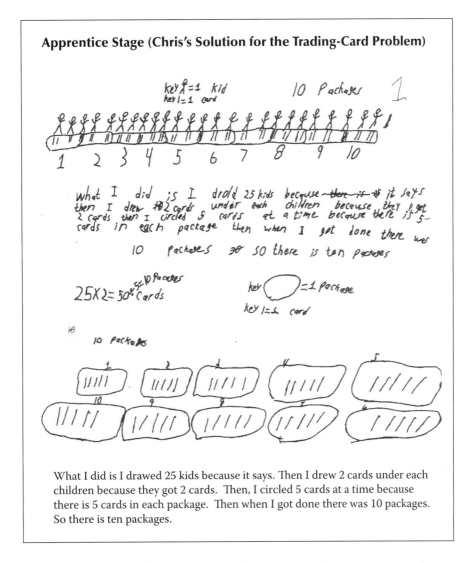

**Apprentice Stage (Chris's Solution for the Trading-Card Problem)**

What I did is I drawed 25 kids because it says. Then I drew 2 cards under each children because they got 2 cards. Then, I circled 5 cards at a time because there is 5 cards in each package. Then when I got done there was 10 packages. So there is ten packages.

Fig. 7.7. An example of an apprentice-level problem solver's solution to the trading-card problem

## Problem Solver

Children at this final stage possess all the characteristics of an accomplished problem solver. They are able to create *personal* solutions for a wide range of problems. They represent their solutions using abstract symbols (e.g., tally marks, number sentences, drawings, lists, tables)

**139**

and can completely describe their solution process by including all the steps used to arrive at an answer. Additionally, they can often solve problems in more than one way. Their thinking is characterized by *conscious competence*—that is, they know why their solution works, and they can explain their logic to others.

### The examples of Ariel, Mckenzie, Timothy, and Dallas

Examples of children at the problem-solver stage in chapters 3 and 4 included Ariel, Mckenzie, Timothy, and Dallas. Those children personalized their solutions to problems, and they confidently described how and why their solution processes worked. They were also able to comment on the strategies used by the other children in ways that showed they understood why those strategies were appropriate or inappropriate.

### Sarah's solution

An example of a solution for the trading-card problem that demonstrates the characteristics of a child at the problem-solver stage is shown in figure 7.8. Sarah used an organized list, which showed that she not only could apply a sophisticated problem-solving strategy but also had good number sense and an appreciation for the relationships within and between the numbers shown in each list. Although parts of Sarah's written description might be hard to understand ("so you need 2 two times 4 packages"), her solution is complete and accurate.

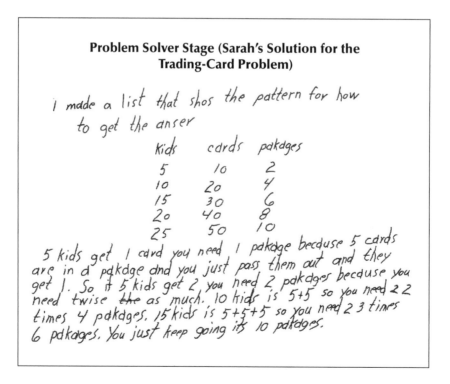

Fig. 7.8. An example of a solution to the trading-card problem at the problem-solver level

# Considerations about the Stages

As teachers begin to notice the seven stages of problem-solving development in their students, the following points may be helpful to keep in mind:

- First, these stages represent general progression in children's development; young children can be at different stages in their development with respect to each of the four descriptors presented in figure 7.1 (i.e., process, product, communication, and reasoning).

- Second, some children may remain at a given stage for a long period of time, as much as a year or more, whereas other children may seem to almost skip a stage altogether.

- Third, children who usually display the characteristics of one stage may revert to a previous stage when solving problems that are especially challenging. For example, children who are functioning at the problem-solver level may need to use manipulatives to solve a particularly difficult problem.

- Fourth, as children move from one stage to the next, they are sometimes unable to solve problems that were easy for them when they were at a previous stage in their development. Some children seem to pass through a state of temporary disorientation as they reorganize their thinking into more sophisticated forms of reasoning. The brain may be going through something similar to the remodeling of a kitchen. During the remodeling process, the kitchen is not functionally usable—it is not the old kitchen it once was, nor is it the new kitchen it will soon be. Kathy Richardson wrote a very interesting article on this phenomenon that appeared in *Teaching Children Mathematics* (NCTM 1997b).

- Fifth, children's development as problem solvers can be delayed or hindered if children are asked to solve problems in ways that lie outside their natural developmental level, for example, being asked to use problem-solving strategies or computational algorithms that they do not fully understand.

- Sixth, some older students (i.e., middle school and high school students) may exhibit the characteristics of children at the concrete or readiness stage—especially if they have not had sufficient opportunity to solve challenging problems. However, given the chance to engage in problem-solving activities, older students usually spend less time at each stage than younger children.

# Helping Children Mature as Problem Solvers

I would caution teachers not to use the stages described in this chapter as a teaching tool to move children through a problem-solving curriculum more quickly. In a problem-solving classroom, teachers should give all children broad and rich experiences at each stage of their development. Then, when children are ready to move to the next level, they will have something solid to build on. I have found that the best way to help children grow and mature as problem solvers is to pose challenging problems, ask the children to share their solutions orally or in writing, and give them feedback in the form of questions or comments about their solutions.

When doing problem solving with young children, teachers sometimes expect beginning problem solvers to display the characteristics and behaviors of novice or apprentice problem solvers. I found that children often struggle with problem solving, not because they lack ability or mathematical understanding but because teachers have unrealistic expectations and do not give them the time and support they need to complete each stage of their development. I am learning that when children are allowed to solve problems in ways that makes sense to them, their natural problem-solving abilities emerge, and when children are given the time they need to develop as problem solvers, their true talents as young mathematicians are revealed.

# 8

# Children Who Enjoy Solving Problems

Understanding is ... important because it is one of the most intellectually satisfying experiences, and, on the other hand, not understanding is one of the most frustrating and ultimately defeating experiences. Students who are given opportunities to understand, from the beginning, and who work to develop understanding are likely to experience the kind of internal rewards that keep them engaged. Students who lack understanding and must resort to memorizing are likely to feel little sense of satisfaction and are likely to withdraw from learning.... Understanding breeds confidence and engagement; not understanding leads to disillusionment and disengagement.

—James Hiebert and others,
*Making Sense: Teaching and Learning*
*Mathematics with Understanding*

We arrive at truth, not by reason only, but also by the heart.
—Blaise Pascal

Nctm's *Principles and Standards for School Mathematics* describes problem solving as the "hallmark of mathematical activity and a major means of developing mathematical knowledge" (NCTM 2000, p. 116). However, in the past many children in my classroom experienced difficulty when solving problems, and they routinely made such comments as "I don't get it!" or " It's too hard!" Now I hear those types of comments less often. Instead, in my classroom I frequently hear "That was a good problem!" (Micah) or "I like the way Sarah solved the problem—it's cool—because it's easier to get the answer" (Darlene).

Like many other teachers who have changed their students' attitudes toward problem solving, I began by first turning to professional resources for guidance. But I also discovered another valuable resource within my classroom—the children themselves. By asking children questions, for example, "Why is problem solving difficult?" I learned that children can offer amazing insights into the intricacies of the problem-solving process and how they learn to become problem solvers.

# What I Have Learned from Children about Problem Solving

Over the past ten years I have documented the comments made by children while solving problems similar to those described in chapters 3 and 4, and as they shared with classmates their solutions to a wide variety of word, or story, problems. Some of the types of problems that we used in our classroom are found in figure 8.1. I have also used one-on-one interviews and discussion groups, such as those described in chapters 3 and 4, to record children's comments and reactions to various classroom practices used during problem-solving activities. In what follows, I summarize what I have learned from children.

---

### Some Types of Problems Used in Our Classroom

**Nonroutine story problems**
- For examples, see the "Problem Solvers" section in the NCTM journal *Teaching Children Mathematics*.

**Problems based on children's literature**
- Without counting the dots on each page, tell how many dots are in the book *Ten Black Dots* by Donald Crews.
- After reading *Slower Than a Snail* by Anne Schreiber and Larry Daste, make a list of comparisons for "I'm faster than ____, but I'm slower than ____"; "I'm taller than ____, but I'm shorter than ____"; and "I'm heavier than ____, but I'm lighter than ____."

**Problems based on classroom events or activities**
- How many pizzas do we need to buy so everyone in our classroom gets 2 slices of pizza, if the pizzas are cut into 6 slices?
- Jacob can walk around the track in 5 minutes. Andrea can walk around the track in 4 minutes. It is 900 feet around the track. If Jacob and Andrea start at the same time, how far will Andrea be ahead of Jacob when she finishes walking around the track one time?

**Open-ended problems**
- The perimeter of Mr. B's garden is 40 feet. What might be the length of each side of his garden?
- There is 55 cents in a box. What coins might be in the box?

**Traditional word problems**
- 6 children share 9 cookies. How much do they each get?
- Jason is 7 years old. How many candles have been on his birthday cakes?

---

*(Continued)*

---

**Some Types of Problems Used in Our Classroom (*Continued*)**

**Problems without words**

- _____  59  52  45  _____  31  24  17  _____
- $12 + 6 = \square + 9$

**Problems authored by children**

- We figured out that one desk is 32 inches long. So how long is a row of 5 desks? But we want to know how many feet, not inches.
- How much more does a paper clip weigh than a piece of paper?

---

Fig. 8.1. Some types of problems used in the author's classroom

# Independence and the Three Ps

*1. Young children want to solve problems, and many children enjoy problem solving more when they can solve problems in ways that make sense to them.*

Taylor, Maria, and other children have taught me about the importance of independence in the process of becoming a problem solver: "I know what I know. I get messed up when I try to do problems the way you (the teacher) want" (Taylor). "The ways on the (problem-solving strategies) chart are hard to remember, and most of the time I get mixed up and I can't decide which one to use, especially when it's a hard problem" (Maria).

In the past I tried to teach problem solving by showing children how to solve particular types of problems in prescribed manners using computation algorithms or traditional problem-solving strategies (guess and check, work backward, look for a pattern, and so on). Now I encourage children to solve problems in ways that make sense to them, and I try to help them acquire the habits, behaviors, and dispositions of problem solvers—patience, perseverance, and a positive attitude. In our classroom we refer to those traits as "the three Ps."

An example of the children's use of the three Ps occurs in chapter 3 when Lindsey and Antonio comment on the process they used to solve a problem involving the area of block H:

> Like, at first we tried to use two of the big triangles (two block Hs) to make them fit on this one (block A). But it didn't work, *so we kept trying until we got it* [italics added]. (Lindsey)

> Then we couldn't get it (be)cause when we put this one (block H) on top of this one (block A), we tried to use ones like this (block C) and they wouldn't work, and *so we tried a whole bunch of them until it worked* [italics added]. (Antonio)

The children practice the three Ps both in their own behavior as problem solvers and in their interactions with one another. An example of such interaction occurred in chapter 3 when Ariel patiently attempted to help Zachery understand her solution to a problem after Zachery commented, "I still don't get it." Ariel looked at Zachery and said, "I can try again. Do you want me to go slower?" Zachery answered, "OK." Ariel repeated her solution, and this time Zachery watched and listened intently to her explanation. Throughout their discussion Ariel made a genuine attempt to patiently assist Zachery and to encourage him to actively engage in the discussion by occasionally pausing and asking him to paraphrase what she had done up to that point.

As I have learned to trust in the natural problem-solving abilities of children, the children have learned to trust in themselves and have developed the self-confidence needed to become successful problem solvers. Chapters 3 and 4 contain numerous examples of children who were eager to solve problems—sometimes correctly and sometimes incorrectly, but always in ways that made sense to them. They were willing to take risks and to publicly share their solutions with others.

When children are given the opportunity to solve problems *their way*, they take great pride and pleasure in developing their own strategies instead of simply practicing strategies they are shown by adults. Ultimately, the strategies that children create often resemble the traditional strategies taught in schools. For example, the children in chapters 3 and 4 solved problems in ways that mirror several traditional strategies:

- estimate (Melissa's "weighing" blocks with her hands; Taylor's estimating the weight of block "corners"),

- use a simpler version (Zachery's thinking of twice 26 as two quarters, or 50 cents, plus 2 cents),

- represent data (Antonio's use of a grid to calculate the area of a block; Andrea's letting nine lines stand for nine trapezoids; Hillary's grouping of eighths to make a mixed number),

- guess and check (Lindsey's guess and check of the sum 7 + 7 = 14; Austin's grouping the number of ounces in various ways to find one that works),

- break into parts (Nicholas's pretending to "cut" a block into pieces ; Ariel's halving an "extra" line to show that half of 5 is 2 1/2; Jonathan's mentally "cutting" hexagons in half to find the number of trapezoids),

- make a list (Brandi's organized pairings of numerals by twos and threes; Dallas's list of the number of hexagons formed by twenty-eight rhombi),

- use a model (Melissa's hand-balance model; Timothy's geometric model for an arithmetic problem involving adding fractions; Andrea's and Jonathan's block-train models to illustrate their thinking),

- look for a pattern (Mckenzie's observation of the pattern of twos when counting the number of hexagonal blocks in trapezoidal blocks),

- draw a picture (Antonio's drawing to partition the quantity 5; Jonathan's drawing to help him count the number of rhomboidal blocks in a hexagonal block; Austin's drawing to partition a hexagon shape),

- use a number sentence (Taylor's "two square sides plus four rectangle sides is six sides"; Mckenzie's "it goes 1 1/2 plus 1 1/2 is 3, …, plus another 1 1/2 is 12"; Dallas's "28 × 1 = 28, …, and 28 × 1/2 is 14 …, so 28 + 14 = 42"; Austin's "Because 25 + 25 is 50 and 3 + 3 is 6, so it is 56 ounces"),

- act it out (Hillary's marking of eights on a ruler to show her thinking), and

- use logic (several children's use of logic in support of their thinking, including Taylor, Nicole, Melissa, Nicholas, Lindsey, Zachery, Antonio, Ariel, Andrea, Jonathan, Timothy, Mckenzie, Austin, Brandi, Hillary, and Dallas).

Children not only create solutions that resemble traditional problem-solving strategies but also invent ways of solving problems that reflect the ingenuity and creativity of young minds. Most children in the classroom, including Jonathan and Timothy, solved the problem "If four hexagons balance the unit block, how many rhombi will balance the same block?" in the manner shown in figure 8.2.

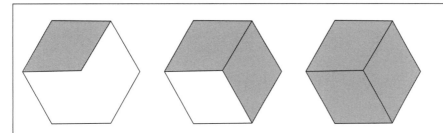

**Most children solved the problem this way:**
- First they placed three rhombi on top of a hexagon so the surface area of the rhombi matched the surface area of the hexagon.
- Then they repeated this action three more times.
- Last, they counted the total number of rhombi used—twelve rhombi.

Figure 8.2. Most children's approach to the problem involving the number of rhomboidal blocks required to balance the unit block

However, one child, Eli, took two trapezoids and said, "Well, these two (trapezoids) make a hexagon, but a trapezoid is really one rhombus and one triangle hooked together like this (see fig. 8.3).

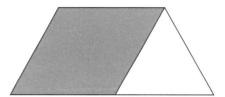

**The way Eli solved the problem:**
"A trapezoid is really one rhombus and one triangle hooked together like this. So if you have two of them (trapezoids), you really got three rhombuses because you count the two (rhombi) you already have and then you hook the two triangles together and that makes another one (rhombus), and so you have three of them (rhombi) in all. But you aren't done, 'cause there are really eight of them (trapezoids), so you do it again and again and again, and that makes twelve rhombuses."

Fig. 8.3. Eli's solution to the problem involving the number of rhomboidal blocks required to balance the unit block

# The Role of Mistakes

*2. Young children want to learn from their mistakes, and many children enjoy problem solving more when they know that their mistakes will be used as stepping-stones to new learning.*

Alexander, Mckenzie, and other children have taught me about the role that mistakes can play in the process of becoming a problem solver: "Sometimes you've got to be wrong so the next time you can be right" (Alexander); "At least I am trying—unlike some kids who don't write anything on their paper and say they don't get it" (Mckenzie). In chapter 3 Nicole is a good example of a child whose behavior shows that she can *learn* from her mistakes as well as the mistakes of others. At the beginning of the activity, Nicole did not seem to understand the problems, and she repeatedly agreed with both correct and incorrect answers offered by other children in her group. However, as the activity progressed, she stopped agreeing with the other children and developed a valid, useful strategy by personalizing the strategy of another member of the group, thereby turning her misunderstandings into a strategy for success.

Chapter 4 contains other examples of children who showed flexibility in recognizing and correcting errors in their thinking. Both Austin and Brandi used the comments of the other group members to fine-tune their solution strategies or correct mistakes in logic. Austin was able to correct a misunderstanding about equivalent fractions, and Brandi deepened her understanding of the process for adding fractional quantities.

I used to teach mathematics using drill-and-practice exercises, and I saw mistakes as a sign of children's failure to remember information or apply information correctly. But now when a child's solution contains an error, I try to remember this little story about the great inventor

Thomas Edison. After Edison made 2000 tries to invent the electric light bulb, a young reporter asked him how it felt to fail so many times. "I never failed once," Edison is reported to have said. "It just happened to be a 2000-step process." Children make lots of mistakes when solving problems, especially when solving problems in ways that make sense to them. But mistakes are a valuable part of the problem-solving process, and both teachers and children can benefit from them:

- Children can use mistakes as learning tools to correct errors in their logic or refine their understanding of mathematical concepts.

- Teachers can use children's mistakes to gain insights into why children make errors, gather information about what children already know, and extend and expand children's existing knowledge.

The following quote about mistakes by the writer and humorist Al Franken is both revealing and enjoyable: "Mistakes are a part of being human. Appreciate your mistakes for what they are: precious life lessons that can only be learned the hard way. Unless it's a fatal mistake, which, at least, others can learn from" (Franken 2002).

Mistakes matter, especially in mathematics, and they shouldn't be ignored. Children need to be made aware of errors in thinking or computation procedures. In fact, my experience has been that children who seem to become the most flexible and adept problem solvers are the ones who most quickly develop the ability to learn from their mistakes. Therefore, I consistently try to reassure children that their mistakes are a natural and necessary part of learning, and as such, are not something to be avoided but rather, something to be embraced. Convincing them is not always easy, because some children see mistakes as a sign of failure, especially if they have experienced mathematics only through drill-and-practice exercises.

Although valuing mistakes is important, equally important is acknowledging the things children do well. Even when a child does not get the correct answer, her or his solution may reveal genuine understanding of the mathematics embedded in the problem (see, for example, the problem and solution in fig. 8.4).

As one child observed, "When I make a mistake, don't just tell me what I do bad—tell me what I do good" (Brandi). As previously noted in chapter 3, many of the mistakes children make are due to the fact that they simply think differently than adults (e.g., Nicole's use of a vertical orientation of the blocks), and the criteria they use to determine the important features of a problem may not be the same as those used by others (e.g., Nicholas's imaginary "cutting" of the blocks into pieces the size of glue sticks; Melissa's unusual, perpendicular arrangement of the blocks). For example, young children frequently arrive at answers to problems that most adults would consider to be incorrect. Also, children often justify their seemingly incorrect answers using a form of logic that most adults find difficult to understand (see, for example, fig. 8.5).

**The problem:**
4 children want to share 14 cookies. How much will each child get"

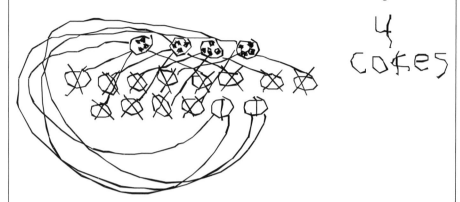

This first grader has solved the problem correctly, as shown in her drawing. However, like many young children, she makes the common error of counting all the dots (cookies) in the circles as whole cookies even though she has correctly cut two of the cookies into halves. When I asked her about the two cookies that were cut in half, she said, "Oh, I needed to cut them in two pieces so each kid got a half of one (cookie) because they are supposed to share, and so they each got three cookies and a half of one, so that makes four cookies."

Fig. 8.4. A first grader's solution to the cookie-sharing problem

**The problem:**

I put 15 red cubes, 9 blue cubes, and 3 yellow cubes into a bag, and I shook them up. Then I reached into the bag and without looking, I took one cube out of the bag. What is probably the color of the cube that I took out of the bag?

Surprisingly, some young children will answer, "yellow." Even more surprising is the reason they give for choosing this color: "yellow because the yellow ones are on the top." These children seem to think that the cubes maintain their relative position in the bag even when you "shake them up," and since the yellow cubes were placed in the bag last, they are"on top" and therefore have a greater chance of being picked. To most adults the important feature of this problem is the number of cubes of each color; however, to some young children the important feature is the relative position of the various colors of cubes in the bag.

Fig. 8.5. The cube-drawing problem and young children's reasoning behind a commonly given incorrect answer

# The Importance of Challenge

3. *Young children want to engage in complex tasks that are completed over extended periods of time, and many children enjoy problem solving more when they experience the satisfaction of overcoming a challenge.*

Comments such as the following from Zachery, Andrea, and other children have taught me the importance of patience and perseverance when solving problems: "It feels good when I finally get the answer, like you scored a touchdown or something" (Zachery). "Sometimes when I can't figure it out, I just keep trying, and when the light bulb comes on in my brain, I go, 'Oh, I get it'" (Andrea).

If the vision of the NCTM *Standards* for mathematics instruction is to be realized, teachers need support and encouragement. Both students and teachers need to learn new roles, behaviors, and skills. Learning to solve problems requires profoundly different ways of thinking and behaving than learning to memorize information. Many teachers feel overwhelmed by the challenge of trying to teach problem solving as a separate topic within the mathematics curriculum, and they need to realize that they can embed the teaching of traditional mathematics skills within the context of problems and thereby teach both traditional skills and problem solving at the same time.

One way to do so is through the use of warm-up activities and minilessons, such as those described in chapters 3 and 4, but teachers can also ensure that the full range of mathematics skills is taught by ensuring that children solve a wide range of problems that cover the entire mathematics curriculum appropriate for their grade level. In most schools the problems that children are asked to solve often address only the NCTM Content Standards for Number and Operations, whereas the other Content Standards—Algebra, Geometry, Measurement, and Data-Analysis and Probability—receive little or no attention. Children can learn and practice traditional mathematics skills through problem solving, but to do so, they need to have opportunities to solve problems based on all the Content Standards (NCTM 2000), such as the algebra and geometry problems discussed in chapters 3 and 4 in this book.

Teachers should ensure that the problems they present to their students address all the NCTM Content Standards and are not limited to traditional word, or story, problems. Problems for investigation can include situations based on classroom activities, events, conversations, and so on (figs. 8.6 and 8.7); "impossible" problems (fig. 8.8); problems authored by the children for their peers to solve (fig. 8.9); and non-paper-and-pencil problems like those described in chapters 3 and 4.

As a further extension of the problems shown in figures 8.6–8.9, children can author their own versions and then solve one another's problems. Problem solving is a complex process, and children need plenty of time to do their best thinking. As one child commented, "I have to think about a problem a long time, and sometimes I need a break to let my brain rest 'cause it starts to hurt" (Antonio).

## The problem:

Hillary is 52 inches tall, and Chloe is 39 inches tall. How much taller is Hillary than Chloe?

Although some of the children's strategies shown below may seem unorthodox and inefficient, they represent children's genuine attempts to make sense of the problem and communicate their solution using a drawing, manipulative, oral description, or computational procedure.

### Jonathan's solution

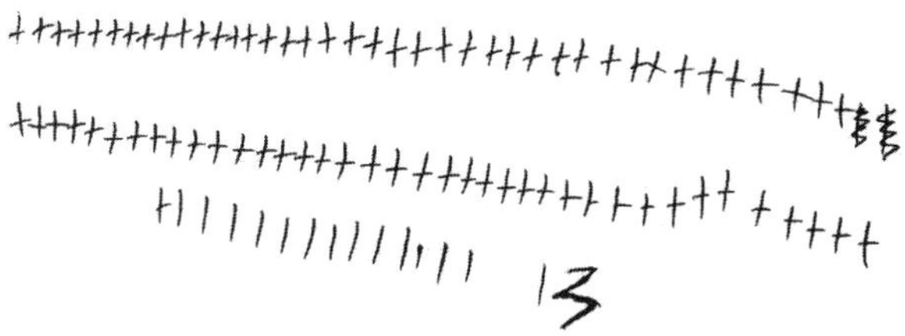

Jonathan first drew 41 lines to represent Chloe's height in inches. He then recounted the lines and discovered that he had drawn 41 instead of 39, so he crossed out 2 lines. Next he drew 52 lines to represent Hillary's height. He then proceeded to cross out one line at a time on Chloe's row and then on Hillary's row. He continued this process until he had crossed out all the lines on Chloe's row. He then counted the remaining lines on Hillary's row and wrote 13 for his answer.

### Andrea's solution

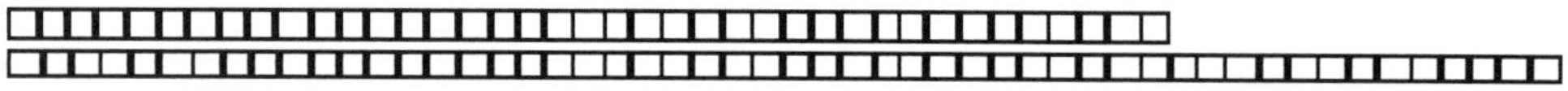

Andrea used a popular classroom manipulative. She made a row of 39 tiles on the floor "'cause they wouldn't fit on my desk." Then she made a row of 52 tiles and counted "the ones that were more 'cause that's how much more she is."

### Alexander's solution

Alexander used a different manipulative than Andrea—his fingers. Alexander put 39 in his head and then used his fingers to count on from 39 to 52. He paused as he reached 49 so he could put "10 in my head for later." When he reached 52, he had held up 13 fingers, so he said, " She is 13 inches more big."

### Natasha's solution

Natasha used an approach similar to the direct-modeling method used by Jonathan, but she had less chance of making a counting error because she used bars to represent the quantity 10. Also, her approach was more accurate than the counting-on method used by Alexander because she did not have to keep track of quantities in her head.

### Brandi's solution

"52 is 40 +12 and 39 is 40 – 1, so it's 12 up and 1 down, and that makes 13."

Brandi used an approach common to some children—a familiar reference point from which to work forward and backward to facilitate her computations. In this instance she chose to use a multiple of 10 so she could "solve the problem in my head."

### Eli's solution

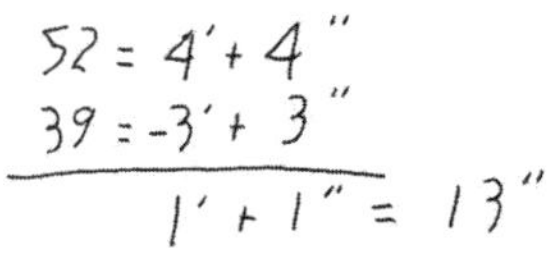

"52 is 4 inches more than 4 feet, and 39 is 3 inches more than 3 feet, so minus them and you get 1 inch and 1 foot, and that's 13 inches."

Figure 8.6. Students' various solutions to the heights problem

# Problem Based on a Comment Made by a Child in the Classroom

Young children love to pose "What if?" type questions in an attempt to stump adults. One day a child posed the question "What if you didn't have rulers, how could you measure stuff?" The next day I presented this problem to the class:

> You need a straw that is 2 inches long, but you don't have a ruler. You have only a straw that is 3 inches long and a straw that is 5 inches long. Using only the 3-inch and 5-inch straws, how could you make a straw that is 2 inches long?

One advantage of this problem is that after children have solved it, they can use real straws and verify their solution.

Most adults would probably solve this problem by placing the two straws side by side, lining up the straws at one end, and then cutting off the section of the 5-inch straw that extends beyond the end of the 3-inch straw, since 5 – 3 = 2.

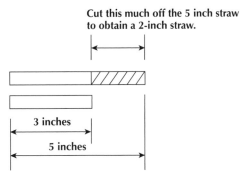

Interestingly, only a few children chose to solve this problem in the manner shown above.

## Kohl's solution
"Glue the 5 and the 3 sticks together at the ends, and break it in half, and then break it in half again and it makes 2 long."

## Zachery's solution
"I know if you put 3 dimes beside each other, it is almost 2 inches but it is just a little bigger, (be)cause Nicole and I measured it the other day when we were doing an experiment. And 2 quarters is almost 2 inches but it is just a little smaller. So 2 inches is in the middle between the dimes and the quarters, so make the straw this long."

## Hillary's solution
"Divide the 3-inch one into thirds, and make the marks on the straw. Count two of them (the marks), and cut it 'cause that's 2 inches."

Fig. 8.7. Children's various solutions to the straw-lengths problem

# "Impossible Problems"

Problem solving often requires creative as well as critical thinking. To stretch children's thinking, I sometimes pose problems that encourage children to play with ideas and to "think outside the box." These problems have earned the nickname "impossible problems" because they appear to lack a mathematical solution.

## How can two children share five pennies?

*Jacob:* You could cut one of the pennies in half and they would each get 2 1/2 cents, but if you cut money in half, it isn't worth anything. So I don't think you can do this problem.

*Chloe:* They could each get 2 so it would be fair, and put the other penny in the bank until they got another 5 cents, and then take the penny out and they each get 3 more cents."

*Ariel:* They could buy a candy bar that costs 5 cents and break it in half, and then they each get half a candy bar and it's a fair share.

*Eli:* They could buy a lottery ticket, and when they win, they could split the $1000 prize, and they would each get $500 and they would be rich forever.

## How can three children share ten balloons?

*Micah:* Well, it's impossible because if you try to cut a balloon in half, it will pop.

*Andrea:* They each take three and give the other balloon to their teacher because he needs to be happy, too.

*Austin:* When no one is looking, let one of the balloons go and say, "Oops, it just slipped," and then share the others so they each get three balloons.

*Timothy:* Sell the balloons for 30 cents, and share the money so they each get 10 cents.

Fig. 8.8. Children's solutions to various "impossible" problems

# Student-Authored Problems with Solutions
## by Other Children in the Classroom

**Brandi's Problem:**
My Mom baked 4 dozen cookies for the bake sale. If there are 6 cookies in each bag and if one person bought 3 bags for $3.00, how many dozen cookies were left?

**Austin's Solution**    **Andrea's Solution**    **Todd's Solution**

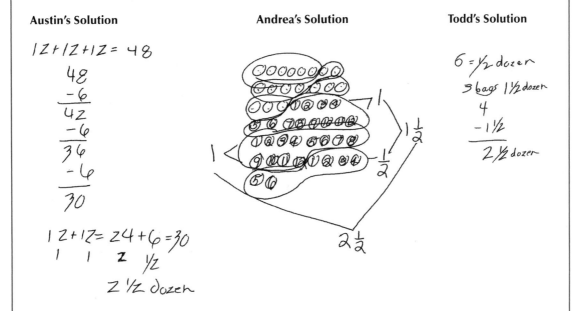

$12+12+12 = 48$

$$\begin{array}{r} 48 \\ -6 \\ \hline 42 \\ -6 \\ \hline 36 \\ -6 \\ \hline 30 \end{array}$$

$12 + 12 = 24 + 6 = 30$

2 ½ dozen

$6 = \frac{1}{2}\ dozen$

3 bags 1½ dozen

$$\begin{array}{r} 4 \\ -1\frac{1}{2} \\ \hline 2\frac{1}{2}\ dozen \end{array}$$

**Zachery's Problem:**
When we went out for pizza, my dad ordered 2 pizzas. My parents ate 3 pieces each of them, and my brother and sister and I each ate 2 pieces. How many pieces of pizza were left?

This is how they cut them

**Hillary's Solution**    **Brandon's Solution**    **Chloe's Solution**

4 peses

$$\begin{array}{r} 16 \\ -3 \\ \hline 13 \\ -3 \\ \hline 10 \\ -6 \\ \hline 4\ left \end{array}$$

4 or fm

Fig. 8.9. Two student-authored problems with examples of classmates' solutions

# The Importance of Discourse

*4. Young children want to communicate their solutions to problems to others, and many children enjoy problem solving more when they can share and discuss their solutions with peers.*

Comments like the following by Nicholas, Melissa, and other children have taught me the importance of discourse when solving problems: "I can understand other kids better than the way you (the teacher) tell us how to do problems" (Nicholas); "I get a chance to find out if they agree or disagree with me, and I get to see how they solved the problem and ask them questions about their answer" (Melissa).

In the past I did not give children the opportunity to share their solutions with one another. Little time was available in our hectic schedule for such a time-consuming activity, and the children really did not have anything interesting to share, because they all solved the problems the same way using strategies I had taught them. Now I realize that for several reasons, young children need a chance to share their thoughts orally:

- Children often learn as much from one another as from me.

- Young children frequently lack the skills to clearly and completely describe their solution process in writing, as reflected in the comment of one child, "Writing about how I got the answer is hard, but I can tell you what I did real easy" (Jonathan).

- Young children become good writers in mathematics after they first become fluent speakers of the language of mathematics. They should nonetheless be encouraged to represent their solutions in writing. I frequently remind children, "Recording your solution in writing not only helps others see how you solved the problem but also helps you do your best thinking." This benefit occurs because students can "use representations to organize their thinking" (NCTM 2000, p. 138) and to help "make mathematical ideas more concrete and available for reflection" (NCTM 2000, p. 137).

# The Importance of Developmental Awareness

*5. Young children want to become problem solvers, and many children enjoy problem solving more when the anomalies in their development are acknowledged by adults.*

Jacob, Lindsey, and other children have taught me the importance of accepting the anomalous nature of children's development as problem solvers through comments like these: "Sometimes I get real smart, and then I can't remember how smart I was" (Jacob). "I don't know how I do it, but all of a sudden I can solve a problem I couldn't figure out before—like, it just hits me like I've been zapped with a smart laser or something" (Lindsey).

I now realize that I must be very patient. The growth of young children as problem solvers is anything but steady and continuous. One of the teachers in our school has characterized this type of development as "bump-bump-jump" learning. Beginning problem solvers often seem to "bump along," and then one day they "jump" to a much higher level of understanding, to the delight and surprise of everyone. Therefore, I have learned to be very patient when children are bumping along. But I have also learned to be prepared for children to unexpectedly jump to a new level of thinking—so that I can maximize their learning and help them jump as high as possible.

## Making Problem Solving Enjoyable for Children

How can teachers make problem solving more enjoyable for children? Although this question has no simple answer, I have found children enjoy problem solving more when they—

- solve problems in ways that make sense to them;

- learn to appreciate mistakes as necessary and valuable parts of the problem-solving process;

- experience the satisfaction that accompanies overcoming an obstacle;

- share and discuss their solutions with peers; and

- receive support and encouragement when their development slows or appears to go into reverse.

By listening to the advice of children, I have been able to create a classroom environment in which children not only enjoy problem solving but also experience a culture of discourse that allows them to grow and develop as problem solvers. I have found that children are natural problem solvers who can solve problems by working alone or in groups. When given the chance to routinely share their solutions with peers, they—

- find ways to communicate their thoughts,

- invent ways to examine and evaluate their ideas before sharing them in public,

- develop techniques to critique the ideas of others and provide useful feedback, and

- develop the capacity to compare different solutions and expand their understanding of the mathematics embedded in problems.

As described in the NCTM's *Principles and Standards for School Mathematics*, "The challenge at this level [K–5] is to build on children's innate problem-solving inclinations and to preserve and encourage a disposition that values problem solving" (NCTM 2000, p. 119). I will continue to rely on children as a resource for clues to unlock their natural talents and abilities as problem solvers. I will also continue to seek out their help in finding answers to difficult questions, such as, "How can I help make problem solving enjoyable for children?" I have come to believe that children find problem solving enjoyable because it is in tune with the way the mind processes information—solving problems is one of the primary functions of the brain—it is what the brain has evolved to do (Sylwester 1995). Therefore, the most powerful learning is not that which teachers etch on the brains of children through memorization and repetition but rather, that which appeals to their hearts as well as their minds. Children need to experience the intellectual satisfaction that comes from solving challenging problems as well as the joy they feel in their hearts when they succeed. If we want children to learn mathematics with understanding, then they must become searchers of the truth—for indeed, as this chapter's opening quote by Blaise Pascal affirms, "We arrive at truth, not by reason only, but also by the heart."

# 9

## Isn't That Interesting?

Problem solving is the cornerstone of school mathematics. Without the ability to solve problems, the usefulness and power of mathematical ideas, knowledge, and skills are severely limited.... Unless students can solve problems, the facts, concepts, and procedures they know are of little use. The goal of school mathematics should be for all students to become increasingly able and willing to engage with and solve problems.

—National Council of Teachers of Mathematics
*Principles and Standards for School Mathematics*

THE SAD RESULT OF TOO MUCH DOODLING DURING MATH CLASS

*P*RINCIPLES *and Standards for School Mathematics* (NCTM 2000) urges, "Students should have frequent opportunities to formulate, grapple with, and solve complex problems that require a significant amount of effort and should then be encouraged to reflect on their thinking" (p. 52). The *Standards* document goes on to say, "Mathematics teaching in the lower grades should encourage students' strategies and build on them as ways of developing more-general ideas and systematic approaches" (p. 76). In short, the Standards expect children to solve *complex problems* in ways that make sense to them by crafting personal solutions to problems. However, when young children solve problems using their own individualized styles of sense making, their solutions may not make sense to others. This situation can create awkward classroom moments that are mathematically challenging and emotionally uncomfortable for both teachers and students.

# Encouraging Emotionally Neutral Language

## Rephrasing student comments

A comment that I often use during mathematics lessons is "Isn't that interesting?" I have found that my frequent use of this positive comment leads many of the children in my multi-age classroom to use it, as well, as they examine, explore, solve, and discuss mathematics problems. It also has the added benefit of replacing children's use of the nonhelpful comment "I don't get it."

In addition, I frequently rephrase a comment made by a child to put a more positive spin on what the child has said. For example, when Antonio commented in chapter 3, "This is hard," I did not ask, "Why is it hard?" but rather, "Why is it challenging?" I have found that children like to overcome a challenge but avoid things that are "hard." Another example from chapter 3 took place when Nicholas said, "This is hard," to which I replied, "I agree, the most interesting problems are sometimes the most difficult to solve, but when you solve them, it makes you feel very good inside because you know that what you have done was special."

## Using "Agree-Disagree" versus "Right-Wrong"

When discussing one another's solutions to problems, I expect children to use the terms *agree* or *disagree* rather than *right* or *wrong*. As the discussions in chapters 3 and 4 show, children become comfortable using the agreement terminology and on occasion even use both terms simultaneously to agree with one part of a solution and disagree with another. I have found that the terms *right* and *wrong* are somewhat emotionally loaded, especially the latter, which seems to shift the focus of the discussion away from the solution process and toward the person who was sharing his or her solution. The comment "You're wrong" seems to carry the message that the person is wrong, not what they have said or done. In contrast, the words *agree* and *disagree* seem to be more emotionally neutral terms. When children say, "I disagree," the resulting discussion focuses more on what the children disagree with (in this instance, the solution to the problem). In addition, the words *right* and *wrong* seem somewhat inappropriate in a problem-solving classroom because the process for solving the problem may be correct even though the answer may be wrong. In classrooms in which children use the words *right* and *wrong*, discussions tend to focus on—

- mistakes children make rather than the things they have done correctly, and

- the answer to the problem rather than the solution process.

Finally, using the phrase "I agree because ..." or "I disagree because ..." forces children to think more deeply about the claims they make. When children—

> are involved in discussions in which they justify solutions—especially in the face of disagreement—[they] will gain better mathematical understanding as they work to convince their peers about differing points of view.... It is important that students understand that the focus is not on who is right or wrong but rather on whether an answer makes sense and can be justified. (NCTM 2000, pp. 60, 198)

## Responding to Perplexing Situations

Elementary school teachers often face a difficult dilemma when asked by a child to comment on a drawing the child has made. Such a situation may not seem like much of a problem to most adults, but teachers of young children realize that commenting on a child's drawing is not a simple matter—especially if you *cannot* tell what the child has drawn. Not wanting to embarrass the child, or themselves, by making a comment such as, "What is it?" teachers use a more respectful response, for example, "Tell me about your drawing."

A similar difficulty arises in mathematics classrooms in which a problem-solving approach is used for mathematics instruction. In this type of classroom, situations often arise that children and teachers find perplexing or confusing. Such outcomes are in sharp contrast with those of classrooms that use a traditional drill-and-practice approach in which the procedures for completing routine exercises are clear and unambiguous—at least to the teacher.

But when children solve problems in ways that make sense to them—rather than practice procedures they have been shown by their teacher—things can become messy both mathematically and socially. When situations like these occur, children and even teachers have a tendency to make such comments as "I don't get it!" However, I have found that a better response to this type of situation is to say, "Isn't that interesting?" The following examples demonstrate that mathematical problems can be challenging for both children and teachers, and at the same time, children's responses to these problems can be very interesting in some unexpected ways.

## Young Children's Thought Processes

### The Pencil Problem

Like many teachers, I have a tendency to assume that children understand the meanings of commonly used words that find their way into mathematics lessons. One such word is the term *each*. Most young children seem to understand the meaning of this word as it applies to situations in which each person in a group gets something, such as a cookie. However, I was surprised by some of the

THE FAMILY CIRCUS—By Bil Keane

"Why are you measuring your feet?"

responses when I presented the pencil problem in its original wording to the first and second graders.

## *Original wording of the pencil problem*

> Melissa has 2 pencils in each hand. How many pencils does she have in all?

Several children said the answer was 2 pencils, and at first I wanted to say, "That's not correct, perhaps you should try the problem again—only this time read the problem more carefully and think about the answer more thoughtfully." Instead I said to the children, "Isn't that interesting? Tell me how you solved the problem."

The children's solution process typically involved modeling the problem for me, since it was apparent to them that more than a verbal explanation would be needed to correct my lack of understanding. These children would lay two pencils on their desk, and then they would pick up one pencil in each hand and say, "See, Mr. B., two pencils—in each hand. Just like it says in the problem." At first I had a hard time understanding what the children were trying to say, since I knew that the answer to the problem should be four pencils. After several attempts to explain to these children that "two pencils in each hand" meant two pencils in both hands, I realized that my explanations were not going to change their minds. Therefore, I did something that some teachers might find strange—I simply ended the discussion by saying, "This is a really interesting problem, and let's all think about it some more and come back to it at a later time."

In classrooms in which accountability and high-stakes testing drive the curriculum, teachers have a tendency to look for a quick fix to correct children's misconceptions. However, I have found that giving children time to ponder a mathematical problem and discuss the problem with others gives them the opportunity to correct their misconceptions on their own and is often more effective than my attempts to teach them the correct answer. Since this advice is also true for adults, later that day I continued to think about the children's responses to the pencil problem and decided to discuss the matter with a colleague. She suggested rewording the problem as follows:

## *Revised wording of the pencil problem*

> Melissa has 1 pencil in each hand. How many pencils does she have in all?

The next day I gathered all the first and second graders and presented them with the reworded version of the problem. When the children finished solving the problem, I asked them to share how they had solved it, and requested that the other children ask questions about each solution or tell why they agreed or disagreed with the answer. Some of the children who had experienced difficulty the previous day immediately became aware of the dilemma raised by this new version of the problem and were able to self-correct their misconception.

Other children refused to let go of their misconceptions and solved the problem by tossing one pencil back and forth between their hands or breaking the pencil in half so that they could hold "one" pencil in *each* hand. However, by the end of the children's discussion, they all agreed that the answer for this problem was two pencils. Although all the children said they agreed with the answer, I knew that some children would need to solve other problems containing the term *each* before they would correct all their misconceptions about this word.

## Time for processing information

I have gradually learned that some children are not always ready to acquire certain concepts on the day I decide to present them. This lesson has been very hard to learn because the traditional teacher inside me wants to ensure that every child understands everything, every day. But the reality is that some children need more time than others to digest all the information that teachers ask them to learn, or they may need more experiences to help fine-tune working definitions of words and the concepts they represent.

Howard Gardener has noted that children form "primitive beliefs" about most things in their world at an early age (Gardner 1993). Those beliefs are highly resistant to change and are modified very slowly over time as children construct new understandings based on experiences that broaden and deepen their knowledge base. Gardner has found that although children can be trained to give the correct answers to questions that teachers commonly ask in mathematics and science classrooms (e.g., What are your chances of winning the lottery? or What causes the seasons of the year?), children frequently continue to hold onto their primitive beliefs well into adulthood even though they are aware that their beliefs are in direct conflict with the correct answers they have been taught in school.

## The Circus Problem

Confusion over the word *each* arose on another occasion, when the first graders were asked to solve this problem:

> Jennifer, her twin brothers, and her parents went to the circus. How much did it cost for the whole family to go to the circus?

**CIRCUS TICKETS**
Children ..................... $2
Adults.......................... $3

Several first graders said the answer to this problem was $5. At first I thought the children had simply added the numbers on the sign in the problem, but in fact when I questioned them about their answer, they had arrived at their solution in a way that I found to be interesting. A typical explanation was "The tickets for the kids (meaning all the children—not *each* child) is $2, and the tickets for the adults (again meaning all the adults—not *each* adult) is $3. So $2 + $3 is $5." Although most of the children in the class realized that the amounts shown on the sign were charged for *each* child and *each* adult, several young children in the classroom—having never been to a circus—were unaware of the usual pricing convention and actually believed that the prices reflected an admissions policy that allowed all children in a family to enter the circus for $2 and all adults in the family for $3.

Unlike in the pencil problem, however, this time I was able to easily clarify the children's mistake. I have found that when children misinterpret information because of confusion over a social convention, as in the circus-tickets example, they respond favorably to direct instruction and more readily accept a teacher's explanation. But when the confusion arises from a misunderstanding of a mathematical idea or concept, as in the pencil problem, children are less willing to abandon their misconceptions. Instead of simply accepting the advice of others, children appear to need to construct this kind of conceptual understanding for themselves.

# Our Unresolved Mathematical Dilemmas

The following problems were very challenging for both the children and me because they resulted in dilemmas that as a mathematical community we were unable to resolve to everyone's satisfaction.

## The Paper-Ghosts Problem

The following problem generated a very interesting discussion in our classroom:

> Brandi made some paper ghosts for a Halloween party. It took her 2 1/2 minutes to make each ghost. How many ghosts did she make in 1 hour?

Two of the third graders each solved the problem in a different manner, as shown in figure 9.1. Both solutions seem to make sense mathematically, and yet each solution produces a different answer. Darlene's solution yields an answer of twenty-four ghosts, whereas Austin's solution yields an answer of twenty-five ghosts.

When these two third graders presented their solution methods to the rest of the class, the resulting discussion did not go as I had anticipated. Instead of focusing on the mathematical validity of each solution, the children engaged in a heated debate concerning the number of answers that are possible for particular types of problems.

All the children in the class were familiar with open-ended problems that can have more than one correct answer, for example, "If I have some coins in my pocket that total $0.25, what coins could I have in my pocket?" The children also realized that some problems, such as the paper-ghosts problem under discussion, should have only one mathematically correct answer. However, because they could not determine which solution for this problem was in error, they decided that a third category of problems existed and offered this hypothesis: perhaps the paper-ghosts problem was a "very, very, very special problem that even though it should have only one answer, somehow it has two answers." They thought that they had made a "great

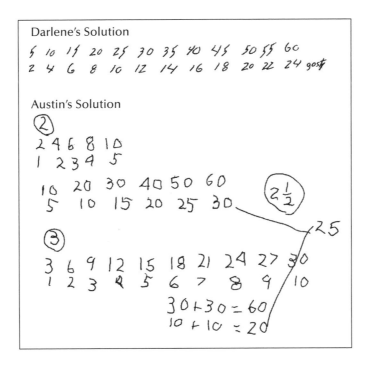

Figure 9.1. Two different solutions to the paper-ghosts problem

discovery" and that we should let the "president and the guys who do mathematics" know about this new kind of problem.

At the conclusion of the children's discussion, all eyes in the room were on me; clearly, they expected me to confirm or refute their hypothesis about the "new kind" of problem. I was fairly certain that the correct answer was twenty-four ghosts. However, I had no explanation for why Austin's answer of twenty-five ghosts was in error. So I said to the class, "Isn't this interesting? I think the answer is probably twenty-four ghosts, but Austin's solution seems to make sense. This is a problem we all need to take some time and really think about."

Although I continue to think about this problem, it has stretched my mathematical understanding to the limit, and I must admit I am still unsure why Austin's solution is not correct. If anyone can offer an explanation that both young children and I can understand, I would appreciate your help.

## The Father-Son Age Problem
Unlike the previous problem, which presented a mathematical dilemma, the following problem resulted in a conclusion that was not only interesting but somewhat humorous:

> When Jacob was 5 years old, his father was 29 years old. How old will Jacob be when his father is 3 times his age?

A typical student solution for this problem is shown in figure 9.2a. However, one child, Eli, noted a pattern that the other children had not seen and decided to continue the list (fig. 9.2b). Eli reasoned that because at one point in time Jacob's father was five times as old as Jacob, and later he was four times as old as Jacob, and still later he was three times as old as Jacob, then if that pattern holds, the time should come when Jacob is one times as old as his father—that is, they would be the same age. The children found this supposition to be very interesting, and I found it to be quite amusing.

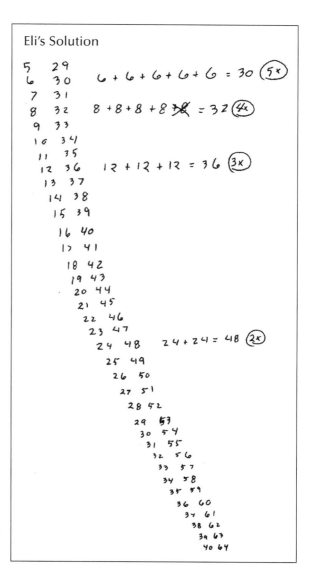

Figure 9.2a. A typical solution to the father-son age problem

Fig. 9.2b. Eli's unusual solution to the father-son age problem

Later I commented to a colleague that the age problem raised all kinds of interesting questions, for instance, "If Jacob's father is five times as old as Jacob today, isn't he five times as old as Jacob tomorrow?" and if this is not true (which the solution to the problem seems to indicate), then "Is Jacob's father aging slower than Jacob, or is Jacob aging faster than his father?" My colleague jokingly responded, "Perhaps this is what people mean when they say that as you get older, you slow down." To which I replied, "Or perhaps it is what people mean when they say that children are growing up faster."

## The Egg-Carton Problem

A common manipulative in our classroom is egg cartons, which the children use for counting, sorting activities, and games, and as aides in solving problems. Some of the egg cartons have been cut into sections with two, four, six, eight, or ten cups. One day while using the egg cartons, a child commented to a classmate, "I just don't get it. You got this small egg carton (fig. 9.3a) and this other egg carton (fig. 9.3b). But the small one is, like, one-fourth smaller than the other one (fig. 9.4), and the big one is, like, one-third bigger than this one (fig. 9-5). It's like they should be the same (one-third or one-fourth), but they're not." The other child replied, "I don't get it, either, but it's kind of interesting. Maybe we should think about it."

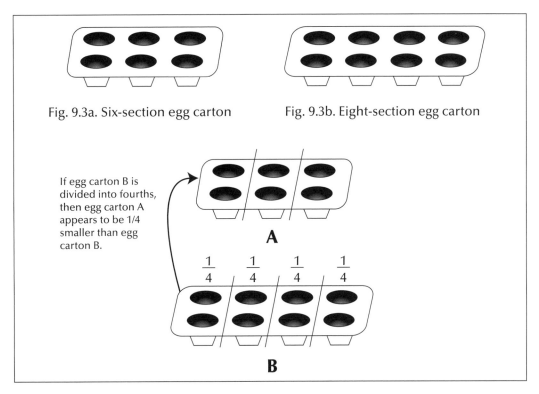

Fig. 9.3a. Six-section egg carton          Fig. 9.3b. Eight-section egg carton

If egg carton B is divided into fourths, then egg carton A appears to be 1/4 smaller than egg carton B.

Fig. 9.4. The smaller carton appears to be one-fourth smaller than the larger carton.

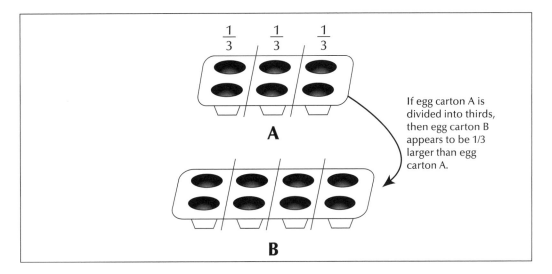

If egg carton A is divided into thirds, then egg carton B appears to be 1/3 larger than egg carton A.

Fig. 9.5. The larger carton appears to be one-third larger than the smaller carton.

As I listened to these two girls discuss their dilemma, several questions entered my mind:

- How could I help them gain a deeper understanding of the fractional concepts represented in this situation?

- Should I let them attempt to resolve the situation on their own, or should I intervene?

- If I do intervene, should I use a direct instructional approach or should I attempt to guide them using leading questions?

- If I do not intervene, should I have the girls present the problem to the rest of the children in the class to see whether the other students can offer any insights into the situation?

All these and other questions confront a teacher on a daily basis when children solve problems instead of completing drill-and-practice worksheets. These questions are not easy to answer, because the answer often depends on the age and mathematical abilities of children as well as the nature and difficulty level of the problems.

# Challenges to the Teacher of Problem Solving

*Principles and Standards for School Mathematics* (NCTM 2000) states, "By allowing time for thinking, believing that young students can solve problems, listening carefully to their explanations, and structuring an environment that values the work that students do, teachers promote problem solving and help students make their strategies explicit" (p.119). During the activities described in this chapter, I allowed time for thinking; I believed in my students and their abilities as budding mathematicians; I listened attentively to their explanations; I created a learning environment in which children took risks and shared their original thinking; and I helped children make their strategies explicit. However, in doing all the things recommended by the NCTM *Standards*, I also created situations that challenged my abilities and exposed my weaknesses as a teacher of mathematics. I discovered that exploring mathematical problems with children can be a messy and unpredictable process that can at times make teachers feel uncomfortable and unsure of how to proceed.

Teachers of problem solving need to have a deep understanding of mathematical ideas and concepts and a thorough working knowledge of the children in the classroom—children's interpretations of the meanings of words, their misconceptions about mathematical concepts, and the kinds of problems that challenge them without being too complex or overwhelming. The whole experience of using a problem-solving approach to teaching mathematics is very *interesting* indeed.

# Dispelling Some Myths about Problem Solving

CALVIN AND HOBBS © Watterson. Reprinted with permission of UNIVERSAL PRESS SYNDICATE. All rights reserved.

A Cherokee grandfather was talking with his grandson when the grandson asked about how he dealt with the anger, struggle, and uncertainties in life.

The grandfather said to him, "I feel as if I have two wolves fighting in my heart. One wolf is the vengeful, angry, violent one. The other wolf is the loving, compassionate, and forgiving one." The grandson asked, "Which wolf will win the fight in your heart?" And the grandfather answered, "The one I feed."

—*Cherokee folk tale*

A BATTLE is being waged in the halls of Congress and many state legislative chambers across America over how mathematics should be taught in schools. The battle is being fought at school board meetings and within professional organizations including the National Council of Teachers of Mathematics.

## How Should Mathematics Be Taught? Traditionalist and Reformist Views

On one side of this battle are the traditionalists, who want to ensure that children learn basic mathematics facts and procedures by being fed a steady diet of drill-and-practice exercises. Proponents of this view point out what they believe is a commonsense approach, namely, that children need to learn the "basics" before they can master more complex tasks. The individuals who espouse this view learned mathematics under that precept when they were in school, and it is how they expect children to be taught.

On the other side are the reformists, who want to ensure that children develop understanding of mathematics by being fed a slightly different diet focused on problem solving. This side points out, "Unfortunately, learning mathematics without understanding has long been a common outcome of school mathematics instruction. In fact, learning without understanding has been a persistent problem since at least the 1930s, and it has been the subject of much discussion and research by psychologists and educators over the years" (NCTM 2000, p. 20). As a result children "who memorize facts or procedures without understanding often are not sure when or how to use what they know, and such learning is often quite fragile" (NCTM 2000, p. 20).

# Children's Attitudes and Beliefs : Outcomes of Intellectual Diet

The outcome of this battle is important because in addition to the intentional consequences that each side tries to promote, side effects also result. One of those side effects might well be the most important issue in this debate: children acquire very different attitudes, dispositions, and beliefs about the nature of mathematics and learning in general depending on which type of intellectual diet is used to provide academic nourishment for their young minds.

## *Outcomes of a drill-and-practice diet*

Children fed a mathematical diet of drill and practice tend to be—

- unsure of their answers even when the answers are correct,

- unenthusiastic about mathematics,

- reluctant to take risks, and

- directed by a kind of learned-helplessness that makes them dependent on others to show them how to complete each new exercise they are asked to practice.

## *Outcomes of a mathematical problem-solving diet*

In contrast, as demonstrated by the children in the preceding chapters, children who are fed a mathematical diet of problem solving tend to be—

- sure of their answers,

- confident in themselves and their procedures,

- willing to take risks and explore new situations, and

- guided by a sense of independence that when fully developed evolves into a kind of *learned helpfulness* toward others.

## The Problematic Nature of Problem-Solving Instruction

*Principles and Standards for School Mathematics* (NCTM 2000) recommends that classroom mathematics instruction needs to be more *problematic*—that is, children need to be given the opportunity to engage in problem solving. Although many reasons can be cited to include problem solving in the mathematical lives of children (Appendix 2), implementation of the NCTM's recommendation to make mathematics more problematic has been difficult to achieve for a variety of reasons, including the following:

- *Problem solving can be hard to teach.* Problem solving challenges teachers mathematically, professionally, and personally. Some teachers lack the mathematical knowledge, instructional strategies, and firsthand experiences needed to teach problem solving skillfully and with confidence.

- *Problem solving can be hard to learn.* Solving problems for which no well-defined routine or procedure exists can be difficult for many children. Children often lack knowledge of mathematical conventions that make problem solving more efficient, lack communication skills that make problem solving more effective, and lack dispositions that make problem solving more enjoyable.

## Entrenched Myths about Problem Solving

The implementation of a problem-based approach to mathematics instruction also has come under criticism because of several *myths* that have grown up around problem solving. Many teachers, parents, and adults hold unwarranted and erroneous beliefs about—

- the nature of problem solving,

- the role that problem solving plays in the mathematics curriculum, and

- the process by which children learn to become problem solvers.

For many adults, problem solving was the low point in their mathematics education, and years later they still remember it with feelings of inadequacy and anxiety. Some teachers hold similar views, and they are reluctant to make problem solving part of the mathematics curriculum. Those teachers are uncomfortable with something they never quite understood when they were students, and they are unsure how to respond when children make comments like these:

- "It's too hard." This comment is unsettling because some teachers think that their primary responsibility is to make learning fun and easy—not fulfilling and challenging.

- "I don't get it." This comment is equally unsettling because some teachers are at a loss as to how to help children "get it" without showing them how to solve each and every problem and thus wind up doing the problems for them.

The myths that have plagued problem solving distort discussions about mathematics reform and undermine the efforts of the reform movement to improve mathematics instruction. Although many of these myths have been challenged by researchers, many adults and some teachers still believe in these misconceptions.

### Myth: Young children cannot do problem solving: it is too complex and requires cognitive abilities that young children have yet to develop.

According to this myth, problem solving is developmentally inappropriate for young children, especially children below fourth grade, as reflected in many of the commercially published books and programs that have been developed to teach problem solving in schools. In fact, "Problem solving is natural to young children because the world is new to them, and they exhibit curiosity, intelligence, and flexibility as they face new situations" (NCTM 2000, p. 116). "Young students can engage in substantive problem solving and in doing so develop basic skills, higher-order-thinking skills, and problem-solving strategies" (NCTM 2000, p. 121).

Recent brain research has revealed some essential factors that influence brain development, one of which is problem solving. In his book *Teaching with the Brain in Mind*, Eric Jensen notes, "The single best way to grow a better brain is through challenging problem solving. The brain is ready for simple, concrete problem solving at age 1 or 2" (Jensen 1998, p. 35).

As can be seen from the discussions recorded in the preceding chapters, young children are quite capable of solving complex problems. Although the children were not always successful, they were adept at what I call *learning-on-the*-go as they modified their existing mathematical understandings to meet the demands of new situations. In addition, the small-group discussions were useful in helping the children extend and expand their existing understanding of mathematical concepts and ideas as they constructed new knowledge from their interactions with peers. These children were not only capable of solving problems but also displayed a high degree of ingenuity and inventiveness, as shown by Melissa's, Antonio's, Andrea's, and Austin's solutions.

### Myth: Before young children can do problem solving, they first must learn the "basics," including computation algorithms and computation facts.

Although this view appeals to many adults, children can learn the "basics" through problem solving, and in so doing acquire factual knowledge that is useful and usable. "Teachers must make certain that problem solving is not reserved for older students or those who have 'got the basics'" (NCTM 2000, p. 121). The pedagogical decision is not an either-or choice that entails abandoning the basics for problem solving. Rather, it is chosing to present more of the basics with understanding and less of the basics as memorization. If children are to learn the basics with understanding, "their mathematics education must include much more than short-term learning of rote procedures" (NCTM 2000, p. 76). In addition, learning with understanding actually makes mathematics facts more useful and usable. "One of the most robust findings of research is that conceptual understanding is an important component of proficiency, along with factual knowledge and procedural facility" (NCTM 2000, p. 20).

For children to do problem solving skillfully, they do need to be taught some basics. For example, they need to be taught the conventions and customs of our society, such as how to write numbers, how to pronounce mathematical terms, and how to interpret the meanings of mathematical symbols. However, as the activities in this book reveal, children can engage in complex problem solving without knowing many of the skills commonly referred to as the "basics." Once children can count, represent their solution, and learn to trust in themselves and their own abilities to make sense of mathematics, they can solve a wide range of problems.

At the top of the list of basics that many people think children should master before they do problem solving is the ability to compute using procedures known as computational algorithms. However, I have found that instead of teaching computational algorithms through drill-and-practice exercises, teaching through problem solving gives children a *genuine* reason to use algorithmic procedures when their own invented strategies prove inconvenient or inefficient. If given the chance, children naturally seek out ways of dealing with large numbers or complex procedures, and one way that makes sense to children is to use traditional computational algorithms.

Asking the question "Which comes first, computation skills or problem solving?" also points out a misunderstanding about the difference between mathematics and arithmetic. Mathematics is a tool for solving problems—it is a way of thinking quantitatively and spatially about things and situations. The ability to think mathematically is what makes problem solving effective. In contrast, arithmetic is a tool for making problem solving more efficient—it is a way of using an algorithm to make computation quick and easy. For beginning problem solvers the ability to think mathematically is essential, whereas the ability to compute is not entirely necessary.

Robert Sylwester, author of *A Celebration of Neurons: An Educator's Guide to the Human Brain* (Sylwester 1995), has commented that the beauty of the human brain does not lie in the fact that it can be made to do things that it has not evolved to do, such as memorizing mathematics facts and formulas. Instead the beauty of the brain lies in its ability to invent things, such as the handheld calculator or computational algorithms, to do those things that the brain does not do well. Likewise the mathematical empowerment of young children lies not in their mastery of mathematics facts and computational algorithms but in their development and growth as problem solvers.

Several of the children in the discussion groups lacked basic computational skills (for example, Nicholas and Melissa in chapter 3) or knowledge of basic mathematical terminology (for example, Andrea and Jonathan in chapter 4). In spite of those shortcomings, they were able to successfully solve problems, participate in group discussions, and deepen their understanding of basic algebra and geometry concepts as the activities progressed.

## *Myth: Problem solving means doing word, or story, problems.*

Word problems are only one type of problem for children to solve, but often they are not the best kind of problem to use with young or beginning problem solvers. When word problems are used to provide practice in the application of mathematical algorithms, they do not engage children in meaningful problem solving. Also, many adults report that word problems were a contributing factor to their development of a fear of mathematics, otherwise known as *math anxiety* (Burns 1998).

Better sources of problems for young children to solve can be found in the context of classroom activities. Children are accustomed to the activities that take place in the classroom, and problems based on such events reflect a sense of reality.

The descriptions of the activities in chapters 3 and 4 clearly show that problem solving does not always mean doing word, or story, problems. The problems described in those chapters were based on classroom events, involved hands-on manipulatives, and were completed in a non-paper-and-pencil environment. The small-group discussions were a natural outgrowth of the children's own discoveries, and helped to reinforce the notion that the children's ideas were valued and useful in determining classroom activities.

## *Myth: Problem solving is best taught as a separate topic.*

This view of problem solving has sometimes resulted in the practice of designating one day of the week, perhaps Friday, as "problem-solving day." In fact, problem solving is a way of understanding and doing mathematics. "Problem solving is not a distinct topic, but a process that should permeate the study of mathematics and provide a context in which concepts and skills are learned" (NCTM 2000, p. 182). "Instead of teaching problem solving separately, teachers should embed problems in the mathematics-content curriculum. When teachers integrate problem solving into the context of mathematical situations, students recognize the usefulness of strategies" NCTM 2000, p. 119).

In our classroom, problem solving is something we do every day—it is the context for thinking about mathematics, it is a set of skills for examining mathematical concepts, and it is a forum for helping children express and share their talents as mathematicians. In our classroom, "[s]olving problems is not only a goal of learning mathematics but also a major means of doing so" (NCTM 2000, p. 52). Problem solving gives children a chance to integrate several mathematical skills as they solve problems and experience firsthand how those skills are related to one another. Problem solving also gives children the opportunity to integrate skills from other content areas, such as language arts, as they share and compare their solutions with peers.

## Myth: Problem solving is best taught as heuristics and problem-solving strategies.

This view has been dominant within mathematics for many years, and it is still advocated by some mathematics educators. Much of the research on problem solving has been based on the assumption that novices should be taught the strategies used by accomplished problem solvers. Many researchers have examined the most efficient and effective way to teach problem-solving strategies to children and have found that middle school and high school students can benefit from systematic problem-solving instruction (Charles and Lester 1982; O'Connell 2000, O'Daffer 1989; Pólya 1957; Reeves 1987; Schoenfeld 1992).

However, a review of the same research also shows that teaching students problem-solving strategies does little to improve their ability to solve mathematics problems in general (Lester 1994; Schoenfeld 1992). When children learn problem-solving strategies using a drill-and-practice approach by simply practicing strategies modeled for them by their teacher, the strategies can become versions of computational algorithms, or what I call "problem solverithms." When children attempt to memorize and remember prescribed strategies for solving problems, their understanding of the process can be as shallow and unthinking as their mechanical use of computational algorithms.

In contrast, some of the latest research on problem solving has shown that children are natural problem solvers who are quite capable of inventing their own strategies (Carpenter et al. 1999; Mills, O'Keefe, Nelson, and Whitin 1996; Trafton and Thiessen 1999). Children can be exposed to traditional problem-solving strategies as another way of solving problems, after they have created their own strategies. Most children readily incorporate traditional strategies into their problem-solving repertoire, or they see them as validation of their own strategies.

An important point to note is that during the discussions described in chapters 3 and 4, I did not help the children craft their solutions to problems by giving them hints, clues, or suggestions about the strategies they might want to use. I did, however, frequently use their strategies—both successful and unsuccessful—as an opportunity to *seize the teachable moment* and provide the children with direct skills instruction. By extending the children's own thinking, I hoped to ensure that any new knowledge the children would acquire would be connected with what they already knew.

## Myth: Boys are better than girls in mathematics and problem solving.

Although traditional mathematics instruction seems to create a disparity in the mathematics achievement of boys and girls, problem solving seems to have an equalizing effect. When an inquiry-based approach is used to facilitate problems solving and when children are encouraged to work cooperatively, girls are more interested in mathematics and their performance improves (Fennema et al. 1998; Hanson 1992; Perez 2000).

Throughout the discussions in chapters 3 and 4, all the children freely shared their ideas with one another, and differences in performance were not attributable to gender. In fact, the central role that communication played in the children's discussion of the problems may actually have worked to the benefit of the girls, because girls at this age sometimes possess more advanced language skills than boys. In addition, the collaborative nature of the activities may have made them more interesting and inviting to girls because girls desire to interact socially with others.

### *Myth: Children are motivated to learn mathematics by competition and rewards.*

Closely associated with the traditional approach to teaching mathematics has been the use of incentives and classroom competitions to encourage children to learn mathematics facts and to complete assignments on time. However, research has shown that competition reduces risk taking, creativity, and a willingness to share with others—three essential ingredients for successful problem solving (Kohn 1986). In his book *Punished by Rewards,* Alfie Kohn makes a strong case for the elimination of extrinsic rewards from schools in general, but rewards and competitions are particularly harmful in problem-solving classrooms in which cooperation and sharing of ideas are highly valued practices.

External rewards are not only harmful in a problem-solving environment, they are often unnecessary. Problem solving can be self-motivating because many children find it to be more relevant, interesting, and stimulating than traditional drill-and-practice exercises or teacher-directed-manipulative activities. When children own the solutions to problems, they take great pride in their accomplishments, and many children enjoy finding new or unique solutions. Also, children take great pleasure in sharing their ideas with one another and experiencing the feeling of accomplishment that accompanies mastering a challenging problem. When children solve problems in ways that make sense to them, they experience the kinds of intrinsic rewards that keep them motivated and interested.

> Students should view the difficulty of complex mathematical investigations as a worthwhile challenge rather than as an excuse to give up. Even when a mathematical task is difficult, it can be engaging and rewarding. When students work hard to solve a difficult problem or to understand a complex idea, they experience a very special feeling of accomplishment, which in turn leads to a willingness to continue and extend their engagement with mathematics. (NCTM 2000, p. 21)

Rather than motivated by competition, the children described in this book seemed to be motivated primarily by a desire to share their thinking with peers and to have others acknowledge the value of their ideas.

## Evolving Myths about Problem Solving

In the cartoon that follows, one of the characters is surprised by the unintended and unexpected outcome that resulted from drawing parallel lines in the sand. Similarly, attempts to introduce a problem-solving approach into school mathematics have generated some unintended and unexpected consequences, including the creation of new myths about

problem solving. Although not as powerful as some of the older, more established myths, these more recent myths sometimes create unnecessary controversy within and outside the mathematics education community.

*Myth: Since most standardized tests do not assess problem solving, children will not do as well on those tests if classroom time is spent on activities other than skills instruction.*

In today's world of standardized testing, this myth has become one of the main reasons given by teachers for not doing problem solving with children. Pressured by parents, administrators, and politicians to ensure that children perform well on "the test," many teachers have come to view basic skills instruction and problem solving as competing objectives. Those teachers believe that when every minute of instructional time counts, emphasizing problem solving takes time away from skills instruction. However, I believe that instruction of mathematics skills is most beneficial, and that children remember skills better, when children learn the skills by embedding them in problem-solving activities. Teachers do not need to sacrifice the development of basic skills to create time in the classroom schedule for problem solving. Competence in basic skills and problem-solving abilities can and should be developed together. In fact, learning skills without the kind of understanding acquired through problem solving makes skills harder to remember.

> Learning with understanding also makes subsequent learning easier. Mathematics makes more sense and is easier to remember and to apply when students connect new knowledge to existing knowledge in meaningful ways.... Well-connected, conceptually grounded ideas are more readily accessed for use in new situations.... (NCTM 2000, p. 20)

As further evidence of the fallacy of this myth, I should note that over the past eight years, only one child in my classroom has failed to meet state benchmark standards for mathematics, even though Oregon has some of the highest mathematics standards in the nation. Finally, Schoenfeld (2002, p. 16) has reported, "On tests of basic skills, there are not significant performance differences between students who learn form traditional or reform curricula"; however, "on tests of conceptual understanding and problem solving, students who learn from reform curricula consistently outperform students who learn from traditional curricula by a wide margin."

## Myth: Getting the answer is still what matters most when doing problem solving.

This view of problem solving perpetuates the belief that solving problems is nothing more than computational exercises cleverly disguised as word problems that can be solved using "key words" or identifying the proper computational operation needed to find the answer. This view of problem solving is shortsighted because problem solving is not just another type of mathematics assignment that children complete. Instead, problem solving is a way of learning to think mathematically. Problem solving is not about just getting the answer, rather it is about recognizing that problems are not really solved until one understands what one has done and why one's actions were appropriate (Brownell 1946). "Surprisingly, it doesn't matter to the brain whether it ever comes up with an answer. The neural growth happens because of the process, not the solution" (Jensen 1998, p. 36).

Some of the people who are the most ardent believers in this myth are the children in our classrooms. Children are too quick to agree with a peer if they have the same answer, and just as quick to disagree if their answers are different. The teacher's job is to ensure that children examine both the answer and the solution process before agreeing or disagreeing with one another. Teachers can help children overcome the tendency to focus on the answers by constantly encouraging children to analyze why a solution to a problem works or why it does not. Children need to be able to answer the question "What is the mathematical concept, idea, or logic that makes the solution of a problem possible?" To further dispel this myth, my experience has been that children frequently arrive at the wrong answer, yet their solution process is correct and their logic is mathematically sound, such as in the example in figure 8.4.

## Myth: The process is more important than the answer.

This myth is similar to the one just discussed, and believers in this myth conclude that if getting the answer is not what matters most, then the process must be more important than the answer. The process used by children for solving problems is indeed important in helping children acquire deeper understanding of the concepts and ideas embedded in problems, and in helping teachers acquire detailed knowledge of children's thinking. The process, however, is not *more* important than the answer—it is *as* important. Answers matter, and especially to those who are inclined to find something to criticize about the mathematics reform movement. Perpetuating this myth weakens the reform movement by making it an easy target for parents and politicians who are critical of what they characterize as "fuzzy math." The children in the discussion groups described in this book seemed to recognize the importance of answers as a quick and easy way to begin their evaluation of one another's solutions, but they also recognized the importance of an understandable and convincing solution process when evaluating the validity of answers to problems.

## Myth: Everybody's right—all answers are equal.

In problem-solving classrooms all answers should be accepted and equally valued, because children will not value one another's ideas unless teachers value the ideas of all children. However, children need to learn to recognize and challenge wrong answers as well as justify correct solutions. Teachers can help children acquire these dispositions by—

- valuing all ideas in a nonjudgmental way,

- demonstrating how to critique ideas without being critical of individuals,

- showing a genuine interest in what children say and do, and

- using probing questions that challenge children to clarify and defend their solutions and answers.

" You do it your way, and I'll do it my way."

Although all answers and solutions to problems are equally valued as representing children's genuine attempts to solve problems, all answers and ways of solving problems are not equal. Children need to learn that some strategies for solving problems are inefficient, whereas others are more effective and can be generalized to solve a wide range of problems. During the small-group discussions, the children and I accepted all solutions as representing legitimate attempts at *sense making*, but we did not accept all solutions as making sense mathematically.

## Myth: Children should always solve problems in groups.

Although cooperative learning is an effective strategy for enhancing the problem-solving environment, children need to have opportunities to solve problems both alone and with others. They need to develop both individual and collaborative skills. Mathematics starts to make sense when children engage in sense making as they—

- solve problems in ways that make sense to them;
- wrestle with ideas and concepts to make them reveal their mathematical secrets;
- share solutions with others and receive feedback; and
- compare their solutions with those of others.

Children do not need to solve problems in groups, but they do need to have the chance to share their solutions with others. "Sharing gives students opportunities to hear new ideas and compare them with their own and to justify their thinking. As students struggle with problems, seeing a variety of successful solutions improves their chance of learning useful strategies and allows them to determine if some strategies are more flexible and efficient" (NCTM 2000, p. 118–19).

Although the children who participated in the activities described in chapters 3 and 4 were working in groups, with the exception of Lindsey and Antonio they did not solve the problems cooperatively. Instead they used the group environment to share solutions, provide feedback to one another, and serve as a sounding board for modifying their personal problem-solving strategies.

## Myth: The best problems for children to solve are now available in commercially published books written by experts.

Commercially published books are one source of good problems. However, many such books contain routine word (story) problems. Better sources of problems are plentiful, and best of all, they are readily available to teachers for free. As stated previously, some of the best problems for young children to solve arise naturally out of the daily activities and events within the classroom. To tap into those problems, teachers need to listen to what children are talking about, and take advantage of the mathematics that engages children as they participate in lunch count, share classroom and playground equipment, explore mathematics manipulatives, investigate Internet sites, and so on.

Perhaps one of the reasons the children in chapters 3 and 4 responded positively to the problems they were asked to solve is that those problems were based on their personal experiences with balances and the discoveries they had made about the blocks. Problems based on activities in the classroom appeal to children and seem more authentic than commercially published word, or story, problems, which may depict situations, events, or circumstances foreign to the lives of children.

## Myth: Problem solving requires lots of manipulatives.

Manipulatives are important tools for children to use when solving problems; they help children make sense of problems and give them a way to represent their solution in a visual manner. Teachers at all grade levels should make available a wide range of manipulatives from which children can select the ones they are most comfortable using. However, the importance of manipulatives has perhaps been overstated, since even young children can learn to represent their solution process using paper-and-pencil drawings or illustrations. Manipulatives seem to be most helpful to children when they are first learning how to solve problems or are solving problems that require the use of a specific type of manipulative (clock, coins, Unit Blocks, pattern blocks, etc.).

Manipulatives played a central role in the activities described in chapters 3 and 4. Not only did I use manipulatives as a visual model for the problems I posed, but the children used them as tools for—

- thinking about problems,

- representing their answers and solution processes, and

- communicating and sharing their solutions with one another.

I should point out, however, that as the children in the discussion groups got older and their problem-solving abilities matured, they tended to rely less on the manipulatives to *speak for them* and instead chose to represent their solution process with a drawing or invented algorithm. Manipulatives can be useful tools for thinking about problems, but the understanding that children need to use them purposefully is not contained within the manipulatives themselves. Children construct that understanding, just as they construct an understanding of the mathematical concepts represented by the manipulatives.

## Myth: Mistakes young children make when solving problems cause bad habits that are hard to break.

Children do make many mistakes when solving problems, especially when they are asked to solve the problems in ways that make sense to them. But those misconceptions persist only if children do not receive constructive feedback. When children are given the opportunity to share and compare solutions with one another, and teachers facilitate those discussions, children receive prompt, personalized feedback. Susan Sowers has noted with respect to the acquisition of spelling skills,

> Like early attempts to walk, talk, and draw, initial attempts to spell do not produce habits to be overcome. No one worries when a child's first drawing of a person is a head propped up on two stick legs. As the errors become more sophisticated—two stick arms protruding from the head where the ears should be—no one fears this schema will become a habit, though it may be repeated a hundred times" (Sowers 1987, p. 62).

I have found the same to be true for the mistakes that children make when solving mathematics problems.

Not only are mistakes not a cause of bad habits, they are important learning tools in a problem-solving classroom. Teachers can use mistakes as a source of valuable diagnostic information about how children think and reason. Also, an incorrect solution process or answer often leads to some of the best classroom discussions. In addition, incorrect answers can be used to deepen children's understanding of a problem by serving as a source for additional problems or versions of the original problem. When a child gives an incorrect answer, teachers can ask the other children, "What problem did this person solve?" Problem solving is not about avoiding mistakes; instead it is about learning from them. "Errors are part of the process of problem solving. If no mistakes are made, then almost certainly no problem solving is taking place" (Martinez 1998, p. 605). Instead of being seen as errors that need fixing, mistakes can be viewed as the first stages of development, and as such they are stepping-stones for adding to what children already know.

The children in the discussion groups in chapters 3 and 4 used their own mistakes, as well as the errors of others, to refine and revise their problem-solving strategies, as can be seen from the descriptions of their conversations. For example, Nicholas refined his cutting-the-blocks-with-a-pen strategy until it worked, and Nicole modified Taylor's strategy to develop a successful approach. In addition, I used the children's errors to generate some of the best moments during the discussions, and to explore more fully important mathematical concepts and ideas.

Albert Einstein (1879–1955) is said to have claimed, "Anyone who has never made a mistake, has never tried anything new." Since problem solving is all about trying new things—finding new answers to new questions in new ways—mistakes will be made. Therefore, teachers need to learn to judge children not by their mistakes but rather by how children handle their mistakes and learn from them.

## *Myth: Problem solvers are lonely voyagers without direct instruction or support from the teacher.*

Although children in problem-solving classrooms are expected to solve problems in ways that make sense to them, they are also expected to discuss their solutions with one another and reflect on the feedback they receive. In fact, in classrooms in which children solve challenging problems, teachers give children a great deal of support and guidance. The assistance they provide, however, is not the kind of help most people associate with the traditional role of mathematics teachers. Instead of telling children what procedures to use to find the answer, teachers in problem-solving classrooms give individualized feedback to children after children have explored problems on their own and have crafted individualized solutions. The goal is to build on what children already know by extending and expanding their existing knowledge.

When children have frequent opportunities to share solutions, they develop very different relationships with their classmates. They start to see their classmates as collaborators, and the leaning process as a social endeavor rather than an individual struggle. When children share and compare, they not only engage in conversations with their peers but also engage in an internal dialog as they attempt to communicate mathematically in ways that others can understand and struggle to understand the thinking of their peers. I have found that two of the major building blocks in children's emerging confidence in themselves as problem solvers are a sense of accomplishment that comes from making sense of problems and a sense of fulfillment that comes from solving problems using sense making.

In our classroom, problem solving has become more than a technique for learning mathematics. When children share solutions to problems and provide feedback to one another with the guidance of their teacher, they are acting not as lonely voyagers but as co-explorers in the quest for understanding. In fact, the true lonely voyagers are the children sitting alone at their desks completing page after page of drill-and-practice exercises.

# Challenging the Myths

The myths that surround problem solving are disturbing, both in how strongly they are held by individuals and in the power they have to distort and pollute the mathematics reform movement begun in 1989 with the publication by the NCTM of *Curriculum and Evaluation Standards for School Mathematics* (NCTM, 1989). Perhaps even more disturbing are how easily those myths are transferred to children and how resistant they are to change. If left unchallenged, those myths rob children of the opportunity to acquire important mathematical abilities, practice valuable life-skills, and experience the feelings of personal satisfaction and empowerment that come from solving challenging problems. However, once children are free of the influence of those myths, their true talents as problem solvers emerge, as can be seen in the behaviors of, and comments made by, the children in chapters 3 and 4, and as reflected in the eyes of Nicholas, Nicole, Andrea, and Austin when they said, "Oh, now I get it," and I knew they truly meant what they said.

# Problem Solving Plus Drill and Practice

**Traditional Drill-and-Practice-Based Approach Leading Up to Problem Solving**

- Counting
- Addition
- Subtraction
- Place-value counting
- Multiplication and division
- Computation with larger numbers
- "Genuine" problems

(Skills are taught in isolation for use later on in solving problems.)

**Problem-Solving-Based Approach for Learning to Be a Problem Solver**

**Meaningful problems with emphasis on—**

- Counting
- Computational operations
- Basic facts
- Place value
- Fractions
- Computation with larger numbers
- Friendly numbers

(Skills instruction is embedded within the context of problems to be solved.)

**Integrated Approach Combining Problem Solving with Drill and Practice**

**Problem Solving**
- Investigations
- Word problems
- Children's literature
- Student-authored problems
- Classroom events

**Drill and Practice**
- Computational exercises
- Calendar activities
- Mental mathematics exercises
- Warm-ups and minilessons
- Homework

# Why Problem Solving Is Important

*Children have an opportunity to learn mathematics with understanding.*

Children who learn mathematics through memorization often lack understanding of the procedures they are asked to practice over and over. In addition, children who memorize procedures find it difficult to go back later and gain a deeper understanding of the concepts underlying those procedures. "When [children] memorize rules for moving symbols around on paper, [they] may be learning something, but [they] are not learning mathematics— knowing a subject means getting inside it and seeing how things work, how things are related to each other, and why they work like they do" (Hiebert et al. 1997, p. 2). In contrast, problem solving is a way of learning mathematics with understanding, because "good problems give students the chance to solidify and extend what they know and, when well chosen, can stimulate mathematics learning" (NCTM 2000, p. 52).

*Children can acquire and practice mathematical skills in the rich context of problem-solving situations.*

Children need practice in mathematical skills, but they should also have a chance to practice mathematical skills in the context of real situations. Problem solving "can serve as a vehicle for learning new mathematical ideas and skills (NCTM 2000, p. 182), and it "can and should be used to help students develop fluency with specific skills" (NCTM 2000, p. 52).

*Children can develop useful mathematical abilities.*

Children who learn mathematics through drill and practice often fail to acquire the abilities to think critically, suggest alternatives, or take risks. "Without the ability to solve problems, the usefulness and power of mathematical ideas, knowledge, and skills are severely limited.... Students who can both develop *and* carry out a plan to solve a mathematical problem are exhibiting knowledge that is much deeper and more useful than simply carrying out a computation" (NCTM 2000, p. 182).

*Children can learn worthwhile dispositions.*

When children learn mathematics through a traditional approach, they frequently develop a form of *learned dependence* because they develop little confidence in themselves or their abilities to make sense of mathematics. Problem solving not only helps children learn to think mathematically but also helps them approach life's challenges with self-assurance. "By learning problem solving in mathematics, students should acquire ways of thinking, habits of persistence and curiosity, and confidence in unfamiliar situations that will serve them well outside the mathematics classroom. In everyday life and in the workplace, being a good problem solver can lead to great advantages" (NCTM 2000, p. 52).

## Children can process mathematical information and make connections among mathematical ideas and concepts.

Traditional mathematics instruction often treats topics within mathematics as separate and unrelated chapters in a textbook. Learning mathematics through problem solving helps children develop understanding that is flexible—knowledge that is adaptable to new situations and can be used to learn new things. Problem solving also results in connected knowledge because it requires children to use what they know to make sense of new information. "Good problems can inspire the exploration of important mathematical ideas, nurture persistence, and reinforce the need to understand and use various strategies, mathematical properties, and relationships" (NCTM 2000, p. 182). Problem solving can also "serve as a vehicle for learning new mathematical ideas and skills" (NCTM 2000, p. 182). "Solving problems gives students opportunities to use and extend their knowledge of concepts in each of the Content Standards" (NCTM 2000, p. 116).

## Children can reflect on their current level of mathematical knowledge.

Traditional mathematics instruction places few demands on children to reflect on what they are learning—their job is to memorize, remember, and recall. In contrast, "Good problems and problem-solving tasks encourage reflection and communication and can emerge from the students' environment or from purely mathematical contexts" (NCTM 2000, p.183). In addition, "Teachers should ask students to reflect on, explain, and justify their answers so that problem solving both leads to and confirms students' understanding of mathematical concepts" (NCTM 2000, p. 121).

# Bibliography

Arrien, Angeles. "Lessons from Geese." Transcribed from a speech based on the work of Milton Olson, given at the Organizational Development Network Meeting for Outward Bound. 1991.

Bach, Richard. *Out of My Mind.* New York: Dell Publishing, 1999.

Baroody, J. Arthur, and Herbert P. Ginsburg. "The Effects of Instruction on Children's Understanding of the Equals Sign." *Elementary School Journal* 84, no. 2 (1983): 199–211.

Blumenfeld, Phyllis C., Ronald W. Marx, Elliot Soloway, and Joseph Krajcik. "Learning with Peers: From Small Group Cooperation to Collaborative Communities." *Education Researcher* 25, no. 8 (1996): 37–40.

Brown, Ann L., and Joseph C. Campione. "Guided Discovery in a Community of Learners." In *Classroom Lessons: Integrating Cognitive Theory and Classroom Practices,* edited by Kate McGilly, pp. 229–70. Cambridge, Mass.: MIT Press, 1994.

Brownell, William A. "The Measurement of Understanding." In *Forty-Fifth Yearbook of the National Society for the Study of Education, Part 1,* edited by Nelson B. Henry, pp. 138–74. Chicago: University of Chicago Press, 1946.

Burns, Marilyn. *About Teaching Mathematics.* White Plains, N.Y.: Cuisenaire Company of America, 1992.

———. *Math: Facing an American Phobia.* Sausalito, Calif.: Math Solutions, 1998.

Buschman, Larry. "Research, Reflection, Practice: Using Student Interviews to Guide Classroom Instruction: An Action Research Project." *Teaching Children Mathematics* 8, no. 4 (December 2001): 222–27.

———. *Share and Compare: A Teacher's Story about Helping Children Become Problem Solvers in Mathematics.* Reston, Va.: National Council of Teachers of Mathematics, 2003.

———. "Windows on Learning: Portfolios, Part III, Taking an Integrated Approach." *Learning* 93 (January 1993): 22–25.

Butterfield, Brian. "Wired for Mathematics: A Conversation with Brian Butterfield." *Educational Leadership* (November 2001): 14–19.

Campanario, Juan Miguel. "The Parallelism between Scientists' and Students' Resistance to New Scientific Ideas." *International Journal of Scientific Education* 24, no. 10 (October 2002): 1095–1111.

Carpenter, Thomas P., Elizabeth Fennema, Megan Loef Franke, Linda Levi, and Susan Empson. *Children's Mathematics: Cognitively Guided Instruction.* Portsmouth, N.H.: Heinemann, 1999.

Carpenter, Thomas P., Elizabeth Fennema, Penelope L. Peterson, Chi-Pang Chiang, and Megan L. Franke. "Using Knowledge of Children's Mathematics Thinking in Classroom Teaching: An Experimental Study." *American Educational Research Journal* 26, no. 4 (1989): 499–531.

Carpenter, Thomas P., Megan L. Franke, Victoria R. Jacobs, Elizabeth Fennema, and Susan B. Empson, "A Longitudinal Study of Invention and Understanding in Children's Multidigit Addition and Subtraction." *Journal for Research in Mathematics Education* (January 1998): 3–20.

Cesarone, Bernard. "Cross-age Tutoring." *Childhood Education* 72, no. 3 (1996): 179–81.

Champagne, Audrey, Leopold Klopfer, and Richard Gunstone. "Cognitive Research and the Design of Science Instruction." *Educational Psychologist* 17 (1982): 31–53.

Charles, Randall, and Frank Lester. *Teaching Problem Solving: What, Why, and How*. Palo Alto, Calif.: Dale Seymour Publications, 1982.

Clements, Douglas H., and Julie Sarama. "Young Children's Ideas about Geometric Shapes." *Teaching Children Mathematics* 6, no. 4 (April 2000): 482–88.

Cobb, Paul, Terry Wood, Erna Yackel, John Nicholls, Grayson Wheatley, Beatriz Trigatti, and Marcilla Perlwitz. "Assessment of a Problem-Centered Second-Grade Mathematics Project." *Journal for Research in Mathematics Education* 22 (January 1991): 3–29.

Cobb, Paul, Erna Yackel, and Terry Wood. "A Constructivist Alternative to the Representational View of Mind in Mathematics." *Journal for Research in Mathematics Education* 23 (January 1992): 2–33.

Devlin, Keith. *Mathematics: The Science of Patterns: The Search for Order in Life, Mind and the Universe*. New York: W. H. Freeman & Co., 1994.

Dewey, John. *How We Think: A Restatement of the Relation of Reflective Thinking to the Educative Process*. Boston, Mass.: Henry Holt, 1933.

Edison, Thomas Alva. http://thinkexist.com/quotes/thomas_alva_edison/ (accessed December 22, 2006).

Einstein, Albert. http://www.brainyquote.com (accessed September 11, 2006).

Falkner, Karen P., Linda Levi, and Thomas Carpenter. "Early Childhood Corner: Children's Understanding of Equality: A Foundation for Algebra." *Teaching Children Mathematics* 6, no. 4 (December 1999): 232–36.

Feldman, Jay, and Peter Gray. "Some Educational Benefits of Freely Chosen Age Mixing among Children and Adolescents." *Phi Delta Kappan* 80, no. 7 (1999): 507–12.

Fennema, Elizabeth, Thomas P. Carpenter, Megan L. Franke, Linda Levi, Victoria R. Jacobs, and Susan B. Empson. "Learning to Use Children's Thinking in Mathematics Instruction: A Longitudinal Study." *Journal for Research in Mathematics Education* 27, no 4 (July 1996): 403–34.

Fennema, Elizabeth, Thomas P. Carpenter, Victoria R. Jacobs, Megan L. Franke, and Linda W. Levi. "A Longitudinal Study of Gender Differences in Young Children's Mathematical Thinking." *Educational Researcher* 27, no. 5 (June–July1998): 6–11.

Fennema, Elizabeth, Megan L. Franke, Thomas P. Carpenter, and Deborah A. Carey. "Using Children's Mathematical Knowledge in Instruction." *American Educational Research Journal* 30, no. 3 (Fall 1993): 555–83.

Fosnot, Catherine Twomey, and Maarten Dolk. *Young Mathematicians at Work: Constructing Number Sense, Addition, and Subtraction*. Portsmouth, N.H.: Heinemann, 2001.

Franken, Al. *Oh, the Things I Know! A Guide to Success, or, Failing That, Happiness*. New York: Dutton Adult, 2002.

Gardner, Howard. *The Unschooled Mind: How Children Think and How Schools Should Teach*. New York: Basic Books, 1993.

Gaustad, Joan. "Building Support for Multiage Education." June 1997. *ERIC Digest* 114. ERIC, ED 409604.

Gorrell, Janet L. "A Study Comparing the Effects of Multiage Education Practices versus Traditional Education Practices on Academic Achievement." Master's thesis, Salem-Teikyo University, 1998. ERIC, ED 424008.

Graves, Donald H., and Virginia Stuart. *Write from the Start*. New York: Signet, 1985.

Gutierrez, Roberto, and Robert E. Slavin. "Achievement Effects of the Non-Graded Elementary School: A Best Evidence Synthesis." *Review of Educational Research* 62, no. 4 (Winter 1992): 333–76.

Hannibal, Mary Ann. "Young Children's Developing Understanding of Geometric Shapes." *Teaching Children Mathematics* 5 (February 1999): 353–57.

Hanson, Katherine. *Teaching Mathematics Effectively and Equitably to Females*. New York: ERIC Clearinghouse on Urban Education, 1992.

Hiebert, James, and Thomas P. Carpenter. "Learning and Teaching with Understanding." *Handbook of Research on Mathematics Teaching and Learning*, edited by Douglas A. Grouws, pp. 65–97. New York: MacMillan Publishing Co., 1992.

Hiebert, James, Thomas P. Carpenter, Elizabeth Fennema, Karen C. Fuson, Diana Wearne, Hanlie Murray, Alwyn Oliver, and Piet Human. *Making Sense: Teaching and Learning Mathematics with Understanding*. Portsmouth, N.H.: Heinemann, 1997.

Hirsch, Elisabeth S., ed.. *The Block Book*. Washington, D.C.: National Association for the Education of Young Children, 1996.

Jensen, Eric. *Teaching with the Brain in Mind*. Alexandria, Va.: Association for Supervision and Curriculum Development, 1998.

Kamii, Constance. *Young Children Continue to Reinvent Arithmetic, 3rd Grade*. New York: Teachers College Press, 1994.

Kamii, Constance, and Ann Dominick. "The Harmful Effects of Algorithms in Grades 1–4." In *The Teaching and Learning of Algorithms in School Mathematics, 1998 Yearbook*, edited by Lorna J. Morrow and Margaret J. Kenney. Reston, Va.: National Council of Teachers of Mathematics, 1998.

Koehler, Mary Schatz, and Douglas A. Grouws. "Mathematics Teaching Practices and Their Effects." In *Handbook of Research on Mathematics Teaching and Learning*, edited by Douglas A. Grouws, pp. 115–26. New York: Macmillan, 1992.

Kohn, Alfie. *No Contest: The Case against Competition*. Boston: Houghton Mifflin Co., 1986.

Lester, Frank K., Jr. "Musings about Mathematical Problem-Solving Research: 1970–1994." *Journal for Research in Mathematics Education* 25, no. 6 (December 1994): 660–75.

Martinez, Michael E. "What Is Problem Solving?" *Phi Delta Kappan* 79, no. 8 (April 1998): 605–9.

Mason, DeWayne A., and Robert B. Burns. "'Simply No Worse and Simply No Better' May Simply Be Wrong: A Critique of Veenman's Conclusions about Multi-Grade Classes." *Review of Educational Research* 66, no. 3 (Autumn 1996): 307–22.

McDermott, Lillian C. "Research on Conceptual Understanding in Mechanics." *Physics Today* 37 (1984): 24–32.

Miller, Bruce A. "A Review of Qualitative Research on Multi-grade Instruction." *Journal of Research in Rural Education* 7, no. 2 (Winter 1991): 3–12.

Miller, William. "Are Multi-age Grouping Practices a Missing Link in the Educational Reform Debate?" *NASSP Bulletin* 79, no. 568 (February 1995): 27–32.

Mills, Heidi, Timothy O'Keefe, Lonnie B. Nelson, and David Whitin. *Mathematics in the Making: Authoring Ideas in Primary Classrooms.* Portsmouth, N.H.: Heinemann, 1996.

Moll, Luis C., and Kathryn F. Whitmore. "Vygotsky in the Classroom: Moving from Individual Transmission to Social Transaction." In *Contexts for Learning,* edited by Ellice A. Forman, Norris Minick, and C. Addison Stone, pp. 19–42. New York: Oxford University Press, 1993.

National Council of Teachers of Mathematics (NCTM). *Curriculum and Evaluation Standards for School Mathematics.* Reston, Va.: NCTM, 1989.

———. *Principles and Standards for School Mathematics.* Reston, Va.: NCTM, 2000.

Nespor, Jan. "The Role of Beliefs in the Practice of Teaching." *Journal of Curriculum Studies* 19, no. 4 (July–August 1987): 317–28.

Newman, Denis L., Peg Griffin, and Michael Cole. *The Construction Zone: Working for Cognitive Change in Schools.* New York: Cambridge University Press, 1989.

O'Connell, Susan. *Introduction to Problem Solving: Strategies for the Elementary Math Classroom.* Portsmouth, N.H.: Heinemann, 2000.

O'Daffer, Phares G. *Problem Solving: Tips for Teachers.* Reston, Va.: National Council of Teachers of Mathematics, 1989.

Pascal, Blaise. http://www.brainyquote.com/quotes/authors/b/blaise_pascal.html (accessed September 19, 2006).

Perez, Christina. "Equity in the Standard-Based Elementary Mathematics Classroom." *ENC Focus* 7, no. 4 (2000): 28–31.

Piaget, Jean. *The Construction of Reality in the Child.* New York: Basic Books, 1954. Original work published in French in 1937.

———. *To Understand Is to Invent.* New York: Grossman, 1973. Original work published in 1948.

Pólya George. *How to Solve It.* Princeton, N.J.: Princeton University Press: 1973 Originally copyrighted in 1945.

———. *How to Solve It: A New Aspect of Mathematical Method.* 2nd ed. Princeton, N.J.: Princeton University Press, 1957.

Pratt, David. "Age Segregation in Schools." Paper presented at annual meeting of the American Educational Research Association, Montreal, P.Q., 1983. ERIC, ED 231033.

Reeves, Charles A. *Problem-Solving Techniques Helpful in Mathematics and Science.* Reston, Va.: National Council of Teachers of Mathematics, 1987.

Rekurt, Martha D. "Peer and Cross-Age Tutoring: The Lessons of Research." *Journal of Reading* 37, no. 5 (1994): 356–63.

Resnick, Lauren B. "Mathematics and Science Learning: A New Conception." *Science* 220, no. 4596 (April 1983): 477–78.

Richardson, Kathy. *Math Time: The Learning Environment.* Norman, Okla.: Educational Enrichment, 1997a.

———. "Too Easy for Kindergarten and Just Right for First Grade." *Teaching Children Mathematics* 3 (April 1997b): 432–37.

Rogoff, Barbara. *Apprenticeship in Thinking: Cognitive Development in Social Context.* New York: Oxford University Press, 1990.

Rogoff, Barbara, and James V. Wertsch, eds. *Children's Learning in the "Zone" of Proximal Development.* San Francisco: Jossey Bass, 1984.

Russell, V. Jean, Kenneth J. Rowe, and Peter W. Hill. "Effects of Multigrade Classes on Student Progress in Literacy and Numeracy: Quantitative Evidence and Perceptions of Teachers and School Leaders." Paper presented at the annual meeting of the Australian Association for Research in Education, Adelaide, Australia, November–December 1998.

Saenz-Ludlow, Adalira, and Catherine Walgamuth. "Third Graders' Interpretations of Equality and the Equal Symbol." *Educational Studies in Mathematics* 35, no. 2 (February 1998): 153–87.

Schoenfeld, Alan. H. "Learning to Think Mathematically: Problem Solving, Metacognition, and Sense Making in Mathematics." In *Handbook of Research on Mathematics Teaching and Learning,* edited by Douglas A. Grouws, pp. 334–70. New York: Macmillan, 1992.

———. "Making Mathematics Work for All Children: Issues of Standards, Testing, and Equity." *Educational Researcher* 31, no. 1 (January–February 2002): 13–25.

Slavin, Robert E. "Synthesis of Research on Cooperative Learning." *Educational Leadership* 48, no. 5 (February 1991): 71–82.

Sowers, Susan. "Six Questions Teachers Ask about Invented Spelling." In *Understanding Writing: Ways of Observing, Learning, and Teaching,* edited by Thomas Newkirk and Nancie Atwell. Portsmouth, N.H.: Heinemann, 1987.

Sylwester, Robert. *A Celebration of Neurons: An Educator's Guide to the Human Brain.* Alexandria, Va.: Association for Supervision and Curriculum Development, 1995.

Thompson, Alba G. "Learning to Teach Mathematical Problem Solving: Changes in Teachers' Conceptions and Beliefs." In *The Teaching and Assessing of Mathematical Problem Solving,* Research Agenda for Mathematics Education series, vol. 3, edited by Randall I. Charles and Edward A. Silver, pp. 232–43. Reston, Va.: National Council of Teachers of Mathematics, 1988.

Thompson, Alba Gonzales. "The Relationship of Teachers' Conceptions of Mathematics and Mathematics Teaching to Instructional Practice." *Educational Studies of Mathematics* 15, no. 2 (May 1984): 105–27.

Toffler, Alvin. *The Third Wave.* New York: Bantam Books, 1980.

Trafton, Paul R., and Christina L. Hartman. "Developing Number Sense and Computational Strategies in Problem-Centered Classrooms." *Teaching Children Mathematics* 4 (December 1997): 230–33.

Trafton, Paul R., and Diane Thiessen. *Learning through Problems: Number Sense and Computational Strategies.* Portsmouth, N.H.: Heinemann, 1999.

Trusty, Edward M., Jr., and Stacey Beckenstein. "A Comparative Study of Single-Graded versus Multi-Graded Classrooms." May 1996. ERIC, ED 417014.

Veenman, Simon. "Cognitive and Non-Cognitive Effect of Multigrade and Multi-Age Classes: A Best-Evidence Synthesis." *Review of Educational Research* 65, no. 4 (Winter 1995): 319–81.

Vygotsky, Lev S. *Thought and Language.* Cambridge, Mass.: MIT Press, 1962. Original work published in 1934.

Watanabe, Ted. "Anticipating Children's Thinking: A Japanese Approach to Instruction." *Mathematics Education Dialogues,* a publication of the National Council of Teachers of Mathematics, vol. 5, no. 1 (November 2001): 3.

Watson, Linda. "Children's Misconceptions and Conceptual Change." *Australian Journal of Early Childhood* 22, no. 2 (June 1997): 12–16.

Wellhousen, Karen, and Judith Kieff. *A Constructivist Approach to Block Play in Early Childhood.* Albany, N.Y.: Delmar Publishers, 2001.

Woodward, John, and Lisa Howard. "The Misconceptions of Youth: Errors and Their Mathematical Meaning." *Exceptional Children* 61, no. 2 (October–November 1994): 126–36

# Additional NCTM Resources for
# Teaching Mathematics through Problem Solving

Readers of *Making Sense of Mathematics* can find additional support for, and information about, teaching mathematics through a problem-solving approach in the following titles from NCTM:

- ***Share and Compare: A Teacher's Story about Helping Children Become Problem Solvers in Mathematics,*** by Larry Buschman (Reston, Va.: National Council of Teachers of Mathematics, 2003). This lively volume is written by an elementary teacher especially for teachers in grades K–5 who wish to implement problem solving in the mathematics classroom. It presents the core beliefs and core practices of the share-and-compare method and describes the four main components of a share-and-compare lesson (warm-up, problem for the day, mathematician's chair, and comparison of solution strategies). The book discusses rubrics and alternative forms of assessment, and encourages teachers to experiment with their own variations and approaches. It includes questions and answers to address concerns that parents may have about problem solving in the mathematics curriculum.

- ***Teaching Mathematics through Problem Solving: Prekindergarten–Grade 6,*** edited by Frank K. Lester Jr. (Reston, Va.: National Council of Teachers of Mathematics, 2003). Helping students make sense of problematic tasks in which the mathematics to be learned is embedded is the goal of teaching mathematics through a problem-solving approach. This helpful guide supports teachers as they pursue such investigations with their students. It explores issues and perspectives, presents classroom problem-solving scenarios, discusses the role of technology in a problem-based approach to teaching mathematics, and presents a research perspective. The volume includes several Teacher Stories that bring to life many of the ideas discussed.

- ***Children Are Mathematical Problem Solvers,*** by Linae E. Saksburg, Melfried Olson, and Judith Olson (Reston, Va.: National Council of Teachers of Mathematics, 2002). This book presents engaging explorations in which children solve challenging problems with significant mathematical content. It features problems from the "Problem Solvers" column in *Teaching Children Mathematics,* complete with solutions and children's work.

Please consult www.nctm.org/catalog for the availability of these titles and for a plethora of resources for teachers of mathematics at all grade levels.

For the most up-to-date listing of NCTM resources on topics of interest to mathematics educators, as well as on membership benefits, conferences, and workshops, visit the NCTM Web site at www.nctm.org.